He ART of the CLO$E

Subtle Selling Strategies inspired by
Neurosciences & Neuropsychology

Raju Mandhyan

INNER SUN
Philippines

the HeART of the CLOSE
Published by Inner Sun,
701, Metropolitan Terraces,
Metropolitan Avenue, Makati City
Philippines, 1200

ISBN-13: 9781515135296
ISBN-10: 1515135292
Copyright © 2016 Raju Mandhyan

Editor:
Luwee Francia *www.wordsmithluwee.com*
Illustrations, Design and Layout:
Raju Mandhyan and Luis De Vera

SPECIAL SALES
All Inner Sun books can be purchased in bulk with quantity discounts for large organizations and, most especially for schools, colleges and other social value-creating organizations. Please reach us for these prices through our website www.mandhyan.com

Dedicated to my friend and mentor, the late Sidney Schindler of New York without whose presence in my life I wouldn't have learned the fine heart of the close.

Dedicated my friends and associates Dean Francisco 'Pax' Lapid, Jojo Apolo, Carlo Calimon, Marites Dimaculangan, Butz Bartolome and Penny Bongato who are on mission to turn Philippines into a country of empowered entrepreneurs.

Dedicated mostly to my loving wife and children without whom I wouldn't have any meaning and purpose to my life.

TESTIMONIALS

As an analytics expert, I am asked quite often about how to use data to drive mores sales. Contrary to what most people expect, I generally suggest focusing more the process of the sale versus some new type of data-driven technology to increase sales. Raju Mandhyan, with his latest book, is right in line with my own experiences on how to be more successful in the art of selling.

Right off the bat, we are prompted by the author to consider the reasoning brain, the romantic brain and the Reactive brain in the sales process. This concept sets the stage for a fresh way to look at the art of selling. Concentrating more on the interaction between buyer and seller, Mandhyan makes it clear that by focusing on a more holistic approach to sales, we can achieve so much more than just closing a sale.

As an avid reader of business books, I found the HeART of the Close a great read and will but it on my book shelf right next some of my favourites like Carnegie, Godin and Kawasaki. The book is full of ideas for the novice and veteran salesperson, solo sellers and big teams alike. It truly is indeed all about the heart when it comes to the art of closing.

Daniel Meyer
President and Founder of DMAI
Decision-Making, Analytics & Intelligence

TESTIMONIALS

Very few authors can blend the amazing insights of NLP with authentic knowledge and experience of sales process to actually simplify the art of closing. Raju's recommended philosophies and practices are priceless. An investment in these has the potential double the productivity of all sales people.

I wish I'd had access to such insights and techniques when I started off. Nevertheless I intend to coach my teams with the technology of the HeART of the CLOSE.

Amitabh Saxena
CEO, Anexas, Europe
www.leansixsigma.co.in

Raju Mandhyan has this exceptional gift and ability of combining wisdom, wit and inspiration that make him stand out from scores of many coaches and mentors I have worked with. This book, the HeART of the CLOSE is a personification of that wisdom, wit and inspiration for the sales person and the sales leader. It is, in short, brilliant!

Antony Thor
Netrepreneur and Director,
Ecoglobal Foundation, Philippines

TESTIMONIALS

Raju's book is unlike any of the selling books as he presents an out-of-the-box paradigm, where all aspects of feeling, thinking and implementing are clearly integrated. The art of the close shows us how to become more aware of others using auditory kinaesthetic, visual and mental faculties. My cognitive and intuitive ability to close deals has heightened after reading this book and thus I am now certain and excited to bring up my bottom-line by selling, in the Raju Mandhyan approach!

Padma Mangharam Siap,
CEO, Creative Magnate Institute,
Cebu, Philippines

The HeART of the CLOSE underscores a natural appreciation for the sales process. More than the "how-to's," I like how Raju's experience and wit weave throughout the book and how simplifies complex concepts.

This amazingly insightful book comes at an opportune time, when the intricacies of selling in this milieu invite a more evolved appreciation for being human than a successful sales person.

This book is a powerful resource for the newcomer and a valuable reminder for the experienced sales professional.

Marie-Paul B. de Luna, PhD
Assistant Dean,
SAIDI Graduate School of Organization Development,
Philippines

TESTIMONIALS

Raju has been a college friend since 1974. For almost 40 years, we lost contact, and in a strange quirk of fate, we got reconnected via Facebook, and met up in Dubai soon thereafter.

A lot of people would write or comment about what Raju has written.

Besides complimenting Raju about the great material he writes, I want to mention a bit about the individual behind his writings.

Having come from very humble beginnings, having seen the major ups and downs and the vicissitudes of life, it is fascinating to see a human being who is a walking, talking example of a lot of the stuff he writes. Additionally, he continues to remain a loving husband, a doting father, a great friend, and a down-to-earth human being.

May his tribe grow and prosper!

Niranjan Gidwani
Deputy Chief Executive Officer
Eros Group, Dubai, UAE

Raju knowledgeably emphasized the importance of coaching to managing sales persons. But more than that he skilfully intertwined the selling and coaching process applying the same engagement tools thus making coaching easier to understand and use by sales managers. Brilliant work!

Arthur Florentin,
Executive Director, Civil Service Institute, Philippines

the HeART of the CLOSE

TESTIMONIALS

I have always known Raju Mandhyan to be an insightful marketing man with an excellent gift of gab. I've also read most of the books he has written which were easy, purposeful read because of the witty and practical stories that re-enforce the learning he presents.

The HeArt of the Close presents itself to me as Raju's culminating work on marketing. It starts with addressing the being-ness of the person wishing to seriously engage in a marketing career, proceeds to the crucial understanding of the evolution from the product to the inclusion of consumer-oriented marketing activities and finally the productive and sustainable growth of marketing results through coaching. I highly recommend The HeArt of the Close as an excellent resource on marketing.

My only concern is how the author will top his own work the next time around.

Sonny Vicente,
Life Coach, Facilitator & Change Advocate

TESTIMONIALS

The Heart of the Close is the most appropriate title for this book. Raju is painstaking in his effort to vividly describe what goes on in the dance between the sales person and the client. We all know the stages in selling but do we understand the minute details that lead to the close? Reading through Raju's book will help you understand how you can add value and sustain a long-lasting, fruitful relationship with all your clients. I really like the book!

Edwin C. Ebreo
President
ExeQserve Corporation

Ultimate reading for the entire sales fraternity. The book has a profound impact on the evolving paradigm for sales. It raises the importance of ecology and other neo-environmental aspects, adding fresh color to enlightened management practice. A beautiful body of work with a heart that inspires!

Raghu Kochar,
Executive Vice President, Corporate Communications,
Fortis Healthcare Ltd.

the HeART of the CLOSE

TESTIMONIALS

As one of the first participants of this seminar, I claim its teachings have been crafted to become rich and will withstand the test of time. The main message of the HeArt of the CLOSE remains strong to this day and that is the needs of the buyer are of prime importance. If a salesperson is focused on this core then all his actions will be planted on solid ground and success will inevitably achieved for the seller, and more importantly, for the buyer.

Raju's way of sharing this concept is amazing and clear. His signature style of intimacy and genuine helpfulness makes the learning experience delightful and practical. The HeART of the CLOSE is a journey to learn and re-learn things of utmost significance and relevance in today's world!

Butz de Castro
General Manager,
MyProperty.ph

FOREWORD

"Close: to shut, exclude, finalize, end…" None of these seems to make sense as a sales goal. Yet the popular word is "Close", so let's redefine it.

"Close: to confirm, commit, make official." What we want to do in a sales relationship is gain official permission to serve our customer; to get the payment so that we can deliver the service or product. To complete the purchase contract so that the process can continue.

The only thing standing between you and your buyer is the act of buying. Once that has happened then the value can be delivered. So why should that be such a tension-filled passage? It needn't be. In this book Raju Mandhyan reinterprets the sales process into its natural components and guides us to use selling as a process of bonding with another person instead of exploiting them. He rightly uses the heart as his metaphor because that's the only part of us that cares.

All other elements of our being are function specific, but the Heart (both the literal and the figurative one) is the Caring Component.

When you care about truly serving your customer, the customer can tell. When you care about them you become a better natural listener. You value what they say, you treat them with respect. These are the most powerful sales skills one can have! A caring provider is almost irresistible to a buyer.

I encourage you to allow your mind and heart to reorganize all that you know about selling. Let the knowledge and skills that you've acquired over the years shuffle themselves into new files that make selling a natural and generous process, one that is centered on being of true service to your prospect. Once this shuffle is achieved you will find that selling comes more naturally for you. Tension will drift away and you'll be more excited about greeting each day of selling.

You will become a resource for good and others will welcome your outreach. So, give Raju your hand for a while and let him guide you to a better path.

In the Spirit of Growth,

Jim Cathcart
Author of Relationship Selling,
Founder of Cathcart Institute,
Thousand Oaks, California, USA
www.cathcart.com

INTRODUCTION

I must confess that I didn't just wake up one morning and discover that I had the ability to sell, influence people's minds positively and then create real value during execution and delivery of promises made.

The process from a distance seemed easy. It seemed all that you had to do was look good and talk good. In fact, I remember one of my bosses sending me off to distant lands with a referral note to potential customers and claiming in the note that the carrier of the letter, yours truly, had the gift of the gab! It took me years, if not decades to figure out that selling and creating value was way beyond being just having a gift of the gab. Selling was and still remains way beyond looking good, listening good and speaking well.

Selling takes imagination, understanding, empathy, patience, open-mindedness, creativity, honesty, commitment, courage and a deep ability to lead, inspire and create value not just for yourself, but for the customer and the world at large.

After years of beating the streets, so to say, when I figured I had acquired a few of those above mentioned skills and competencies I plunged into a journey of learning the elements of fine communications, human behaviour and the dynamics of diverse businesses in the marketplace called the world.

To teach, train and coach others into these principles and practices I dove headlong into the fields of neurosciences, neuropsychology and discovered how they were all so related and intertwined. How efforts in one area would impact and improve human performance in another area and eventually into the marketplace.

This book waited years to be born and I must confess the labour pains were severe and excruciating. Now, as I lay my eyes on this finished product I feel like bits and pieces of experience, wisdom and the hidden sciences of success that lay in my bone marrow and my heart have taken form.

Thus, I place this HeART of the CLOSE on the table for you, the reader, to feast upon and then go put on your super sales-person cape and create value in this beautiful world.

Raju Mandhyan
June 2016, Philippines.

TABLE OF CONTENTS

THE CAST

Buy-side

Sell-side

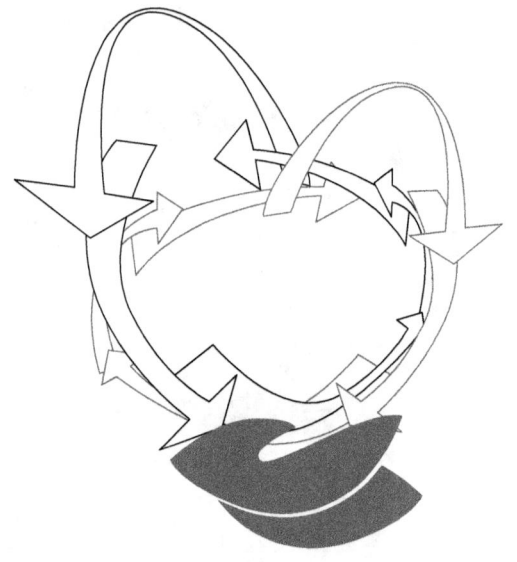

CHAPTER 1

SELLING TODAY

Gone are the days when sales people had to be snappy looking, fast talking, and bag-toting musketeers. Gone are the days when mere product knowledge, industry experience, terrain familiarity and the right connections could land you a sale. Gone too, are the days when buyers were taken in by the name of a brand, the flash of a product and the ease of making the purchase. Especially gone is the time when professional selling was a one-way street called Pitch, Push or a Closing Cul-de-sac.

Today, the selling profession has transcended its former negative image of a racket run by fast-talking, glib-tongued characters. Today selling is a relationship, a collaboration; a dance where who is leading whom is not easily discerned. Selling today is a journey of equals whose destination is value creation. It is a destination that is constantly moving. It is a progressive goal into a far off future.

Close What?

Yesterday's managers and supervisors frequently prodded their salespeople toward increased sales and productivity through mantras called "Always Be Prospecting" and the ABC of selling, which meant "Always Be Closing." My question to these folks had always been "What do you mean always be closing?" Closing what?

But isn't that stating the obvious? Isn't it apparent what the statements, "always be prospecting" and "always be closing" are saying? Isn't any sales person or any individual for that matter, always prospecting or closing? Isn't life itself about having and filling needs? Aren't we, humans, always on the lookout for things to live by, grow with, and build upon? Isn't life a constant struggle up the Maslowian Mountain of needs?

In highlighting and pushing these two paradigms of "always be prospecting" and "always be closing," we have taken our focus away from what is important in life. Life is about learning, loving and living out our innate desires as human beings to create value in the lives of others.

Thus, I would like us to take a second look at and reconsider our perspective of the word "close," which is of hunting, capturing, and feeding only our own needs. I would like to reintroduce "close" in a perspective of being near, being open, supportive and trusting. I'd like to propose "close" as an act of coming together to co-create value for the world through the hearts of our collective minds.

the HeART of the CLOSE

WHY THE HEART?

Well, the word heart is symbolic of the core where precious trust and shared values reside. These values need to align, to get close and have a productive relationship.

People's buying decisions are made from the heart.

Beyond the symbolism of the word heart, it is extremely important to know what research has proven. People's buying decisions are made from the heart. The final yes or no often transcends all logical and rational analyses. What it comes down to is actually a cocktail of emotions and primal needs. That is why some people store up goods that, actually, serve them no discernible purpose. Take for example, shoes and bags for women; cars and hair products for men. That is similarly why many, sensible solutions in businesses are not accepted or acquired; because the group's intellectual, emotional and primal needs did not come to a consensus.

Allow me to walk you briefly through the halls of neuroscience. As I walk you down these corridors I will simplify jargon and blend the nuances of art and science to arrive at outcomes relevant to the selling profession.

THE REASONING, THE ROMANTIC AND THE REACTIVE BRAIN

Let's start by acknowledging that every part and cell in our body constantly sends signals to the human brain. These sensory inputs to the brain are never inactive or dormant. As long as

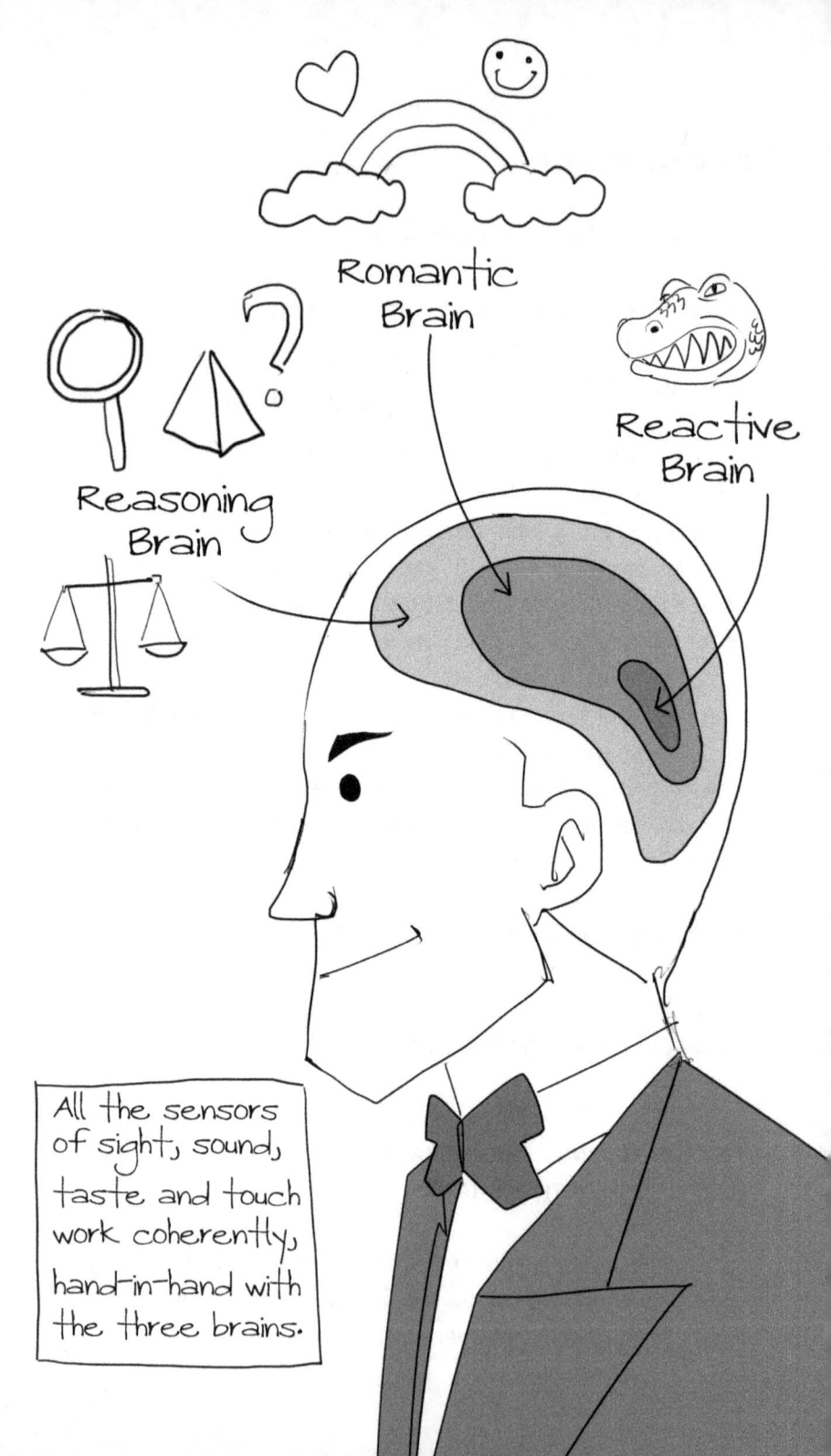

Romantic Brain

Reactive Brain

Reasoning Brain

All the sensors of sight, sound, taste and touch work coherently, hand-in-hand with the three brains.

we are alive, these sensory inputs are in constant touch with this three-and-a-half pound lump of grey matter in our skulls through the modalities of seeing, smelling, hearing, tasting and touching.

Besides having a left or right hemisphere-dominant thinking, it is also made up of three shades of gray. These three gray shades or layers have been called by many names. High school science books called them the cerebrum, the cerebellum and the brain stem. Other books referred to them as the outer, the inner and the primitive brain. For purposes relevant to sales and to making business decisions, let's call them the Reasoning Brain, the Romantic Brain and the reigning Reactive Brain.

The Reasoning Brain absorbs facts, figures and features of a product. Its job is comparing, contrasting and number crunching. The Romantic Brain takes into account past experiences, hearsay and others' opinions and blends it all with imagination and hopeful expectations.

The Reactive Brain looks and waits. It is in constant touch with the screaming and streaming reports of sight, sound, smell, taste and touch. It churns these organic, non-quantifiable data while eavesdropping on the conversations between the Reasoning and the Romantic brains.

For a purchase transaction to take place, this Reactive Brain has to give the final approving nod. Be aware and note that by the metrics of human evolution, this Reactive Brain is thousand-fold older than the Reasoning Brain and the Romantic Brain

Thus, if an individual needs to make a positive commitment towards a decision and then take action, then all the sensors of sight, sound, smell, taste and touch work continuously, hand-in-hand with the three brains until a nod of approval is received from the Reactive Brain.

Do also take note that the Reactive Brain is millions of years old and probably doesn't understand English or Arithmetic. It is also home to three major decisions we constantly make–the decisions to freeze in fear, take flight from crisis or stay and fight against odds.

CHAPTER 2

TWO ULTIMATE TRUTHS ABOUT SUCCESS IN LIFE

INTENTION IS THE DRIVER

Through the buzz going on in our brains plus the billions of cells actively receiving reports and sending out commands, important decisions have to be made: decisions about life, about business and about future growth. These choices become the cornerstones from where we propel our life and move forward. The clarity, quality and strength of these decisions determine the success of our businesses and our lives.

Successful sales and business people credit the quality and frequency of their successes to their clear, firm decision-making in life.

How about luck you ask? I call it, not luck but rather, circumstantial probability and chance.

The process of making clear, deliberate, quality choices and

Intention is not merely a desire or a choice but a strong determination by the three brains to struggle on, to succeed and co-create.

then anchoring all effort and expectations onto this choice is called Intention. Intention is not merely a desire or a choice but a strong determination by the three brains to struggle on, to succeed and co-create.

Let me now further explain the source and the soil in the system from which powerful intentions spring forth and explode into our worlds.

The source of our intention is our true identity. It is not the façade we put up or the convenient roles we play in life to show the rest of the world. Our identity is that deep response to the question, "who am I?" It is a hodgepodge of our past starting from our genetics, DNA, character traits, education, experiences and everything now surrounding us. Identity goes deeper than being Irish American born in California with forefathers from Ireland. That is just a small aspect of "who am I" because every single Irish-American grows up and assimilates learning processes in a uniquely different way. Several other characteristics then add up to make the single dynamic and constantly evolving human being that is you. This past comprises the first part of your identity which, in time, leads you to your true, powerful intentions.

The second aspect of manifesting intention is the soil in the system. It is the kind of environment that surrounds you, a dynamic ecology in a world of changing economies. This breathing and changing world has an impact on you and who

The birthing of intention is the
Reactive Brain's war-cry backed up
by the Reasoning and Reactive Brains
to succeed to win, to excel.

you are, in the same manner earth, wind and fire would impact the strength of a blade of steel. This environment, ecology and economy can harden, corrode, and melt you down. Or, it can strengthen you and your self-image.

Think of the birthing of intention as the Reactive Brain's war-cry (backed up by the Reasoning and Romantic Brain) as it claims its place in the sun and struggles against the environment, the economy and constantly changing circumstances. Intention then is this powerful, never ending struggle to achieve your goal and fulfil your dreams.

Only Action is Measurable

Now, all the dreaming and yearning of the three brains will amount to nothing unless the Reasoning Brain teams up with the Romantic Brain to clean out smudges and survey the terrain with a clear vision of the final destination. The dream will remain a yearning until The Reasoning Brain and the Romantic Brain draw out a plan and take action, step by step and measure by measure, towards that desired destination.

Most of us have dreams and desires but we are often so tied up in our old habits, attachments and circumstances, and dreams remain just dreams. Unless we get off the fence of uncertainty and lethargy and take real action, nothing will come of those dreams.

In sales as in life, we have to be willing to jump off into the darkness of possible unsafe grounds to achieve something and get somewhere. We have to take action steps no matter how seemingly shackled and unsteady our feet are. We must climb

the HeART of the CLOSE

Measurable action,
succesful or
otherwise, is the
the manifestation
of our dream's
clarity and passion.

and claw our way using all possible tools and resources. Mental and physical action need to be taken to get to where we want to be and reach our fullest potential.

Among all the processes our three brains perform—the dreaming, articulation of our wants, and planning–none is more visible and measurable as action. Furthermore, taking action is not a one-time mission but a daily practice. Our actions may deliver negative results some of the time. We may lose accounts and experience failure or even bankruptcy. Whether positive or negative, these outcomes will always be considered measurable results of action.

These measurable outcomes of our actions, successful or otherwise, are the manifestation of our dream's clarity and passion. They are measurable outcomes of our creativity with planning and consciousness in execution. These outcomes affirm the alignment or lack thereof among our Reasoning, Romantic and the Reactive brains.

CHAPTER 3

FIVE FUNDAMENTALS OF ALL SUCCESSFUL INTERACTIONS

Successful selling skills are a reflection of good interpersonal skills. Every sale achieved is an outcome of assessing, approaching and navigating multiple interactions between a salesperson and her buyer. Manage and master your ability to connect, engage and ethically influence a prospect and he will become your customer for life.

Research from several schools of thought has revealed fundamental practices followed by great communicators in managing their interaction with people so that a large percentage of their conversations rake in success and wealth.

ONE: CLEAR PURPOSE AND OBJECTIVES

An old fable about Socrates narrates thus. He was one day walking the streets of Athens when an acquaintance ran up to him and shouted, "Socrates, Socrates! I have something to tell you about Demosthenes. It's real juicy stuff!"

Socrates held up his hand and gestured for the man to stop and cool down. "Tell me," he says, "the thing that you're about to tell me about Demosthenes, is it a fact? Is it the truth and were you personally witness to it?"

Flabbergasted the man splutters and stops in his tacks, "No, I wasn't personally a witness to it; I just overheard some folks down the street talking about it."

A crystal clear purpose along with well thought out objectives will take away anxiety and doubt in how you communicate.

"Well then, in that case," responded Socrates, "will the content of this juicy stuff do you, me or Demosthenes any real good?" His friend literally sank into the ground he was standing upon and muttered, "I'm not sure I... Uh, I don't think it will benefit Demosthenes, you or myself."

"So let me understand," said Socrates, "you don't know if the story you're about to tell me is the truth and neither will it benefit you, me or Demosthenes. So, what exactly is your purpose in wanting to share this juicy stuff with me?"

Socrates' acquaintance then lowered his head shamefully, backed away several steps and quickly disappeared into the crowded streets of Athens.

The point of the story is whenever we indulge in talk and

conversations prior to creating noise with our mouths, we must carefully reflect upon what we are about to say, why we want to say it, and what positive outcome we hope to generate from the conversation.

Good communicators and effective salespeople are crystal clear about their messages. They spend time researching, reading and pondering upon what to share and ask customers and partners and where to direct their conversations. Think before you speak. First, think through what you want, why you want it and what it is you might create.

A crystal clear purpose along with well thought out objectives will take away anxiety and doubt in how you communicate. It will build confidence and discipline towards achieving positive results in business.

TWO: ENHANCED AWARENESS AND SENSORY ACUITY

Growing up in India, I went to a Zoroastrian School. It was a good school and as with most schools, it had all kinds of teachers. Some were nice and some not so nice. Some were passionate about their work and some regarded their work as just a job.

I remember them all, the stuff they taught us and the way they taught us. As I now train, facilitate and coach others in personal and organizational development, the subject of learning and the quality of learning transfer often comes up.

We had this very special teacher who we called D.N. Iran at the Sardar Dastur Hoshang Boys' High School.

D.N. Irani had a remarkable way of teaching, behaving and carrying himself when he traversed the corridors of the school. He was tall and lanky, with very little fat on his body. He wore his salt-and-pepper hair closely cropped and was always clean shaven. He was about the size and shape of Clint Eastwood, as Clint Eastwood looked in his fifties. In a light blue short sleeved, bush shirt with khaki chinos and soft brown leather sandals he seemed to serenely glide from classroom to classroom, to the library or the faculty room.

When approached in the corridors or in class D.N. Irani never seemed hurried or tense; he always heard everyone out fully before he responded. No sounds, no momentary movement or novelty in his surrounding would make D.N. Irani flinch. He remembered faces and the conversations he had with those faces even if all the faces of the boys in a highly populated Indian school looked much alike. In this school with its reputation of toughness, D.N. Irani walked tall and spoke slowly but always carried a big stick of subtle influence. The boys would part in the hallways to let him pass, like Moses' Red Sea, although nothing in his attitude or behavior demanded such from the boys.

Whenever other teachers or even the school head master were faced with a hooligan crowd in class they would always send for D.N. Irani to come and bail them out. And D.N. Irani never failed at quieting down a class simply by turning up and planting himself in silence. In the middle of all storms his mere presence would, somehow, make everyone see the brighter side of life.

What is it that D.N. Irani did for him to be so respected and revered in the tough Sardar Dastur Hoshang all-Boys High School?

the HeART of the CLOSE

1. Enhanced Awareness
2. Start with a clean state of mind. Watch closely and carefully. Note details.
3. Listen in, beyond words, to pitch, to power, to pauses, etc.

4. Feel and take note how you are impacted kinaesthetically.

5. Integrate all data to assess well.

> when he looked at you, he saw all of you, in appearance and in demeanour. When he listened to you, he heard everything you said and everything else you were trying to tell him.

D.N. Irani had presence. He was grounded and totally at ease with himself. When he looked at you, he saw all of you, in appearance and in demeanour. When he listened to you, he heard everything you said and everything else you were trying to tell him. He rarely interrupted and did not jump to conclusions while watching and listening to you. He never passed judgment about people and their issues until he had gotten maximum information. He was never hasty or mad about expressing his point of view. And when spoke, his expressions and opinions were unequivocal and stated in simple, direct language with a mellow tone to his voice. Even when his statements were not in your favor, you always felt he gave due respect to your individuality and humanity.

Today as I look back, I am more and more convinced D.N. Irani's sense of sight, hearing and kinaesthesia (which is a combination of feeling, touching and smelling) were razor sharp. He cognitively and deliberately made efforts to always keep his senses alert, alive and empathetic.

You see, everything we are, think and do is devised, developed and deployed by our five senses. Researches and scientists talk

about genetics—our DNA and our traits—as codes in our birth cells transferred from our parents. These codes may be in chemical or energy form but they're all accessible and recognizable through appearances, sounds and behavior. They are also referred to as visual, auditory and kinaesthetic codes.

Everything we learned from the time our mothers conceived, carried and nurtured us has been written and is stored in our brains using these codes. From our formative years through our youth, and into our adulthood, everything we experience and everyone we interact with happens through the function of our five senses. Our knowledge, values, principles and belief are all stored in our memories. An inventory of this storage is maintained in the format of our five senses and a combination of these five senses.

In his classic book, How to Think like Leonardo Da Vinci, Michael Gelb talks about Artescienza—the art and science of improving the quality of our thinking. Michael Gelb suggests we improve vision by studying art, landscapes and beautiful sights. He recommends listening to classical music, sounds of nature, inspiring speeches and creative stories to sharpen our sense of hearing and our minds. To improve our sense of taste, smell and touch, he encourages activities that alternatingly soothe and stretch these senses, thus strengthening and sharpening them.

Stronger and sharper senses improve our ability to think and we become more aware and sensitive to other people and to our surroundings; therefore, improving our ability to interact with our world.

Individuals like my former teacher, D.N. Irani, knew this at an intuitive and cognitive level. Perhaps they had no chance to

AUTOTELIC
• Thoughts
• Words
• Action

EXTERNAL INPUTS
• Sights/Visual
• Sounds/Auditory
• Taste
• Touch
• Smell
• Kinaesthetic

INTERNAL INPUTS
• Memory
• Synthesis
• Decisions

explain these paradigms they lived by, but they became living examples of this acute awareness and practice.

Here are five practices to enhance your sensory acuities, heighten your awareness and improve your ability to live in the moment;

- Start with a clean state of mind. If any recent visual, auditory or kinaesthetic experience is on your mind– perhaps an unappealing sight you have just witnessed, a song humming in the back of your mind or the scent of pungent food- then consciously let go of the experience using the Reasoning Brain. Let them all be erased from the desktop of your mind.

- Enhance visual acuity. Whenever you see an object, ponder a bit more on its shape, size, and color. Think of it as visually studying something in detail. You can also practice this when observing human facial expressions.

- Enhance auditory acuity. Listen to music and distinguish the sounds of the different instruments involved. Make an effort to mentally dissect the high notes and the low notes of the piece. Do this when listening to another person. Listen for pitch, power, percussion, pauses and the parlance. It'll help you better discern messages they may not be actually verbalizing.

- Enhance your kinaesthetic acuity. When for example, you carry a puppy; feel his weight, his fur, his nails, his bones and all the features that make up a puppy. Feel his body temperature, the moisture or the coarseness of his fur. Pay attention to his smell and breathing. Note how of all this impact your thinking and feeling towards the puppy. This also works well when you are in the presence of another person. Take note of the person's presence, skin-tone, scent and how all this impacts your feelings and opinions about this person. You might have heard the statement, "there's something fishy about him." It doesn't mean he smells like a fish. It means his presence, behaviour, and communication gives you an uneasy, suspicious feeling.

- Integrate the data gathered from all sensory inputs when dealing with others. When talking to strangers, notice how their appearance and the quality of their voice make an impact on you. Observe how their scent influences your impressions. Tally all the data from all these sources, but be aware the impact on you does not truly represent them. Let the Reasoning Brain double-check and assess all data objectively.

Enhancing sensory acuity is firstly, about becoming conscious of all the inputs and noting their impact on our three brains and secondly, about cognitively segregating the useful from the non-useful data. Sensory acuity can store up good knowledge and wisdom in the triune brain. High quality cognitive knowledge and empathetic wisdom will turn us into D.N. Irani, a person of subtle influence and power.

Finding Quiet Ground as a Person

Our five senses actively and constantly absorb, process, filter and store new data in our memories. This buzz of activity combined with old existing data and expectations of the future keeps our state of mind in a frenzied edge all the time.

Having a high amount of unmanaged activity inside our minds

the HeART of the CLOSE

1. Shut-out all non-related thoughts.

2. Assess and settle in into the meeting room ambiance.

3. Become quiet. Pray.

4. Turn your attention to your breathing until it calms down, becomes rhythmic.

5. upload an old, happy memory until you smile.

in comparison to the sounds and events on the outside make us unnecessarily anxious. Conversely decreasing the amount of unmanaged activity inside our minds in comparison to the sounds and the events on the outside will keep us cool and composed.

Finding quiet ground will result in a well-managed, well-controlled state of mind regardless of the quantity and quality of noise and activity on the outside. This well managed, calm control is a direct function of the Reasoning Brain driven by the prefrontal cortex of the brain. It is as if the Reasoning Brain is cautioning the Romantic Brain to wind down its bubbling romantic expectations and soothing the Reactive Brain from its fear driven fantasies.

To achieve and sustain a calm, sensible state of mind, we must frequently slow down the Reasoning Brain, relax the Romantic Brain and soothe the Reactive Brain.

Great salespeople have the ability to deliberately control their state of mind, cool it down and make it highly sensitive to every sound, gesture and change of emotion of a prospect. It is a good ability to have and a great place to be, spiritually. It makes us proactive and productive through every possible shift in the sales interaction.

Here are some tips to getting grounded before and during sales meetings.

    a. Shut out all thoughts about incidents that might have occurred before the sales meeting. In the training industry it is like "parking current questions" during classroom interactions. In a regular meeting it can benefit us when we "park away" active unrelated thoughts not relevant

the HeART of the CLOSE

to the meeting at hand.

b. Take in the meeting room, the venue and every sensory input that might impact your thinking. Then, bring focus away from what can sabotage the quality of your interaction with your customer.

c. Those who believe in the power of prayer may say a brief, private prayer. The resulting outcomes are phenomenal.

d. Those who trust the mind-body connection may close their eyes for a short while and turn their attention to their breathing, taking soft, even breaths to quiet down their state of mind.

e. It also helps to transcend into a positive, happy memory from the past about having successfully handled similar selling situations. The good memory will cool your nerves and let you settle in.

Do what works for you. This process of finding quiet ground doesn't have to be confined to just one time or only to sales meetings but can be practiced every time and through all exchanges in life. It is being in harmony and influencing harmony onto the environment.

Managing Perceptual Positions

Finding and maintaining this calm, quiet ground in any sales situation (when you have a good grip of your thoughts and emotions; you observe well, hear everything better and become a better judge of exchanges) means you have managed your own self, your own position. This quiet management and control of your own state is referred to as an enhanced First-Person Perspective— yours. It's a good place to be in when interacting with others.

A step higher than this fully aware state of mind is to place yourself in the Second-Person Perspective. What is the Second-Person Perspective and how does it work?

In his highly acclaimed book, The Seven Habits of Highly Effective People, author Stephen Covey, describes an incident. A person riding a New York subway finds himself in the same compartment with a man whose handful of kids were creating a ruckus, causing ire to all the other passengers on board. The father of the kids sat with his head held in his hands, oblivious and seemingly unaware of the disturbance his kids were creating. The first person standing not far from the father thought it was rude and careless of the seated father to let his kids carry on with such conduct. In his mind, he built several negative opinions about the father's character. When he could no longer bear the noise of the kids and his own irritation at the father, he walked up to the man and said, "Excuse me, sorry to say this but your kids are creating a huge ruckus and it is impolite and discourteous of you to let this occur in a public place such as this subway." The seated man looked up and, seeming to come out of a reverie, said "Oh, I am extremely sorry! I was lost in my own thoughts and I didn't notice. You see their mother just passed away this afternoon and I don't know how to break the news to them and how to go on in life." Upon hearing this, the complainant felt shame and guilt for his presumptions about the character of the father.

The Second-Person Perspective is a way of managing your mind in such a way that you hold yourself back from jumping to

the HeART of the CLOSE

conclusions or making any assumptions, (especially negative ones) about the other person's character or intentions. Yes, you observe gestures and watch with increased visual acuity. Yes, you listen well, deeply hoping to understand, know and assess your customers' needs and expectations. But you do not make conclusions. The feelings that come up in you about other people are yet to be verified and validated. Treat all assessments and feelings as data and not evidence for us to make a final judgement. Make the effort to be in their position. Think about what they might be thinking, feel what they might be feeling… in their shoes.

Holding back judgment was something teacher D.N. Irani did well back in Sardar Dastur Hoshang Boys High School. Every boy in the school somehow sensed and felt respected by him. He earned not just popularity but more importantly, the trust of the boys. D.N. Irani had immense power and influence to change things for the boys because he knew about empathy and how to place himself in the other person's shoes. This approach is known as the second-person perspective of managing state.

The third perspective is easy to comprehend from our handle on the first and second person perspectives. The Third-Person Perspective of managing state is that of being a mentor or a coach to yourself.

How is this done? It's a matter of exercising our imagination and modelling someone we regard to be a great communicator and someone we look up to. The First-Person Perspective is being cool, calm and collective through fluctuating emotions and changing circumstances. The Second-Person Perspective is keenly observing, listening, and sympathizing with the other person by putting ourselves in their shoes and not being judgmental. In the Third-Person Perspective, we detach ourselves from the First-Person [us] and the Second-Person [them] and mentally float into an imaginary hologram of our role model, our coach or whoever we consider to be wise and a great communicator. From within the hologram of this person, we watch and observe how we, ourselves, think, behave and speak. It's like having an imaginary coach observing our every move to guide and inspire us to do better and to lead us into excellence.

This technique is also similar to the creative-visualization practiced by many successful athletes, actors and writers with every move, every nuance to improve their craft. In the same manner that it is used to achieve excellence in physical and creative performance, we can also, as salespeople, use it to improve business results.

In the first few attempts, it may feel awkward and clumsy but with some practice, it becomes a catalyst for what is known as unconscious competence in the field of skills and talent development.

The Five I's of Mindful Listening

At this point, I'd like to take you a bit deeper into the act of listening. It is a universal truth that good listeners make great thinkers and great thinkers make powerful and persuasive communicators. The process is cyclical and self-sustaining. When we communicate well, we think well; and to think well we need to learn to listen actively and deeply. I will go further and add that the act of deep listening makes us great communicators, leaders, salespeople and value-creating agents of change. Many people talk about listening with the mind

and the heart and listening with the mind and body in tandem. I now add listening with the full attention of the Reasoning brain, the Romantic brain and the Reactive brain. Furthermore, when we listen to others we must listen with a willingness and readiness to change our opinions and ourselves.

The core function of the 21st century salesperson is to create value, provide solutions and build partnerships with the customer, while always considering the customer's needs in any situation. How can this be possible if we are unwilling to change our stance and opinions in life and at work?

In school we are taught how to read, write and recite but have any of us spent time learning to listen fully with our mind? If we learned to listen with our head and our hearts combined, we'd be able to manage our time better and manage plans and projects more efficiently

Putting our heads and hearts together makes us not just attentive but also watchful of our own input into communications. In my workshops, this habit is called Listening Mindfully.

The benefits from listening mindfully:
- Recognizing your authenticity and making you aware of your intentions.
- Enhancing your relationships with your customers, colleagues and the community.
- Giving you the capability of bringing about meaningful, positive outcomes for your customers.

The 5I's to Mindful Listening are:
1. **Investigate intentions.**
   Before entering into any conversation, find out

what it is you really want to achieve. An honest appraisal of your intentions will keep you open and interested in new ideas. Before going into any meeting, I mind map my own thoughts, ideas and expectations. Mind mapping is a type of thinking, brainstorming and organizing technology created by Tony Buzan.

2. Increase Awareness.

While you are listening, clear your mental clutter. These could be nagging thoughts, a list of tasks to do and plans for the day. Postponing such thoughts increases awareness and allows you to learn more. Take note of any change in tone, pitch and pace of the speaker. Look for underlying feelings in the words being uttered. Visualize your mind storing information in key words and images just like in mind mapping.

3. Interact with Interest and Enthusiasm.

Listening is not done just with your ears. It is also done by your eyes and body. Maintain eye contact and lean in towards the speaker. Every now and then blink with approval, nod, smile or participate gently by uttering words like "uh -uh" "hmmm" "gee!" or "wow!" Keep this participation genuine and gentle. Recognize, note and accept your own change of emotions.

4. Inquire and Paraphrase.

All transfer of information, knowledge or ideas from one mind to another generally leaves a small

the HeART of the CLOSE

percentage of a gap of the unknown. Clarify and fill that gap as much as possible by making simple, direct, and un-offensive questions. Rephrase ideas or create metaphors to further solidify understanding.

5. **Inscribe Impressions.**
This is possible in meetings or conferences where more than three people are involved and they have to take turns at communicating. The quick, colorful, note-taking feature of mind mapping will help you put down your impressions and will later allow you to review ideas and perceptions at a glance.

Following these five simple steps will help you enhance your listening skills. Improved listening skills will help you absorb more, clarify more, and make better creative and conscientious decisions about people, issues, and situations. Listening mindfully will also sustain you in such a state that you will be active, empathetic and have the 'willingness to change,' to be flexible.

THREE: RECOGNITION AND RESPECT FOR DIVERSITY AND CHANGE

It's sad enough that the world is broken up into so many geographical parts. We have drawn lines of differentiation from the North to the South Pole, from the East to the West. Our beliefs, ethnicities and cultural mindset further influence our attitude and treatment of others, putting them into stereo-typed segments. Effective and successful leaders must strive

the HeART of the CLOSE

to rise above all this murk. They have an open and supportive mindset backed by immense tolerance for other people who do not reason, romanticize or react to issues the way they do.

Although the human brain is divided into the three functional segments of reasoning, romanticizing and reacting, every single one of us is a unique individual because of different DNA permutations, diverse backgrounds, and variances in education and experience. Unfortunately, societal programming leads us into generalizing and stereotyping people at first glance. Effective and successful leaders respect diversity by accepting that people are different. Their behaviour is simply different; not necessarily bad or worse than our own uniqueness. In addition, leaders and good salespeople profoundly recognize that human circumstances and perspectives are in a state of constant flux. Perceived realities vary and these realities change from moment to moment all the time.

A buyer who shows interest in your product on Monday morning may suddenly have a shift in his circumstances and could change his mind on Tuesday afternoon. The ultimate reality is: different realities and they are changing all the time. It's easy to say "different strokes for different folks" or "the only constant in this world is change" but it's totally another matter to live out these truths. To succeed across diversity and constant change, we must live out these beliefs and practice open-mindedness, flexibility and adaptability… all the time.

In the world of neurosciences and its application to work, there exists a respected group of consultants who do not at all use the word "is" when describing another person in their communications and interactions. Why? They believe what "is" means to the speaker is simply that particular speaker's perspective; not solid fact. What "is" today may not be what "is" tomorrow. Everything and everyone is always changing.

Respecting diversity amongst people is a challenging habit to live out and practice. Yet it can grant us the power of being a super sales performer and human being. With this habit we can become active learners, early adapters and resilient Samurais of interpersonal skills in every sales and selling interaction. It keeps our proverbial "saw" eternally sharp and smooth so it can cut, softly and subtly, through the hardest of challenges.

In the following paragraphs, we will talk about how this resiliency will help us with Zen-like renunciation from short-term results and instant gratification, which are common expectations in the business of selling.

Becoming keenly aware, grounded and present in the moment are all activities of self-management. These activities are crucially important for leading in sales interactions.

For us to transition attention from "me" to "we" and from "us" to "them," it is important for our buyers to see our positive objectives for them. They need to establish trust in us, in our abilities and i intentions for them. Only then will they start believing we want to find solutions together and create value for them.

We have already begun working on presence by clarifying intentions and feeling from the second-person perspective principle as stated earlier. To get a good second-person perspective, we need to know about our buyers' industry, type of business, business model and customer market. All this information can be researched through books, reports, financial

the HeART of the CLOSE

statements and from online libraries. Beyond this general data, we must also gain true, relevant information direct from the horse's mouth. But for the horse to be motivated to speak they need to trust you; and to increase your trustworthiness, you need valuable insights into their businesses and personalities. It's a catch-22 of sorts–a catacomb.

Valuable insights into the buyer's industry and business are the key in working through this catacomb. We must be able to learn quickly, deeply and with the desire to innovate products, improve processes, and raise profits for clients.

FOUR: EAGERNESS AND ABILITY TO LEARN AND INNOVATE

Years ago there was this humorous story about an inept salesman selling Bibles across the small towns of America was going around the internet. It's a great story and puts across the point of eagerness and learning.

This Bible salesman would knock upon the doors, mumble his way through his introduction, stumble through his presentation and make an overall mess of what was considered to be an easy sale back in the day.

Upon seeing his inadequacy at his job, most of the people answering the door would get frustrated at his approach and respond with,

"You don't know a thing about selling, do you?"

"No, ma'am, not really! I am new to this job and also quite

The reversal of this attitude and the desire to learn creates a good vacuum that draws the buyer in to where solutions can be created.

clumsy around it."

"Oh, you nitwit you, there's nothing tough about selling, you know!"

"Yes, ma'am, you're absolutely right. I need to trust that fact."

"Oh, come now," they'd rebuke, "let me show you how."

And, the customer would then go about teaching this nitwit of a salesperson how to sell correctly. Well, at the end, you guessed it. His sales multiplied and he often made it to superstar status in his company.

His approach might be considered tricky today, but the essence of the Bible salesperson's story lies in our wanting to learn. When your buyer senses and is convinced you want to learn about them to help them improve, then they often lean over backwards and hand you their trust in spades.

My belief is this 'wanting to learn' is about innate curiosity. This desire to learn and add value is the anti-thesis, the opposite of what has been considered a standard selling process. In the standard selling process, the seller shamelessly shoves features, advantages and benefits to the prospective buyer. The reversal of this attitude and the desire to learn creates a good vacuum that draws the buyer in to where solutions can be created.

I massively trust and profess success from the process of inquiry and questioning at any time and place. This is the process of diagnostics and counselling that community workers, therapists, and doctors utilize. It is the process of interacting, learning and understanding our clients prior to prescribing solutions. Interacting, inquiring deeply to learn about the customer is the true **Heart of the Close**.

The 5R Questioning Tool Box

The HeART of the CLOSE calls for the softer and smoother side of selling. The process of questioning, learning and helping with the Five R questioning tool box is the answer.

Let me begin explaining this idea by raising a question: What do you think happens inside a person's mind when we ask her a question?

She responds? She begins to think? She feels like filling in the vacuum created by the question asked during the conversation? She begins to think?

Okay, well, what exactly is thinking?

Might thinking be an inward rummaging through of former experiences and stories stored in the Reasoning, the Romantic and the Reactive brain?

Yes?

Well, uh, okay. What does she do inside her head after she has rummaged through the three brains for possible fits to the conversational vacuum?

the HeART of the CLOSE

She picks the best responses to the questions raised in the conversation, you say?

That is correct. Then what does the person do, in her mind, with those best choices?

Structures them?

Oh, you mean organizes her thoughts to put together a cohesive and a comprehensible response?

Does she, then, wrap those goodies up in a proper language form?

Yes, she does, huh?

Now, after she has delivered these choice goods assembled by her mind with the help of the three brains, what exactly is her relationship to the nicely bundled response?

Oh, unclear is it?

Let me put it this way, how does she feel about what she has just articulated?

She feels responsible (for) and towards it.

Good!

Now let me pause a bit from this probing. You see the act and the process of questioning sparks thinking, curiosity and co-creation by the one who raises the questions as well as the one who responds to them. Not only does it co-create thought, it also perks up the levels of engagement to heady

the HeART of the CLOSE

heights. After these high levels of engagement from these conversations taper off, the respondents are led into becoming accountable for their responses. The process generates a sense of ownership and commitment to those ideas that have been offered and co-created.

In our day-to-day lives, good doctors use a lot of questions. Teachers and parents empower their young ones by challenging their minds with questions. Counsellors and therapists bring about healing and recovery through a process of careful and compassionate inquiry. Business leaders drive innovation in their businesses by questioning and challenging the status quo.

"Ask not what your country can do for you; ask what you can do for your country," was the challenge of John F. Kennedy which sparked a new dawn of nationalism and love for country in Americans. Successful and effective salespeople sell solutions, address challenges and serve their customers by gaining insights into these customers' needs and cultures. A careful questioning process is the answer to a powerful selling success.

We now have a basic understanding of the process of inquiry and the value behind asking questions. After we go over a few more basics, this book will take you deeper into the process of inquiry for effective selling.

The basic questions are the open and closed questions. Open questions encourage thinking and possibilities. Open questions generate divergent and creative thinking. These questions help you understand your respondents' mindset and business needs. Closed questions generate narrower, limited responses. Both are broad categories that teach us about questioning to empower, construct and develop solutions. As we get into the actual toolbox, we will also run through how they spark off divergent thinking and convergent thinking.

So let us agree that questions create increased engagement and empowerment, whether they are open or closed and whether they start with what, when, who, where, why, which or how. Let us also glance at how questions can move from being closed to open and then on to increasing empowerment.

For example:

From: Do you like this product?
To: Describe what you appreciate about this product.

From: Can we come to a conclusion about this project?
To: What other factors are you still considering for us to move ahead?

From: Are you ready to make the purchase?
To: How can we help you acquire this service?

In the above examples, you will notice how moving from an ordinary question to an improved one creates thinking space for the respondent. Ordinary questions can terminate the exchange of ideas while the latter can continuously synergize.

With these insights into the process of correct questioning let's now look at the 5R Questions. They give form to **the HeART of the CLOSE** and turn it into a practical science.

R1-RESEARCH QUESTIONS

These are questions that help us generate large quantities of

the HeART of the CLOSE

raw data about our customers business, product, industry and specific business model. These questions probe big windows of opportunity for us to see beyond the front of the store, so to speak, and to understand the internal set up of the customer's business. These questions subtly work toward building rapport and discovering areas of possibilities between the customers' needs and the services we provide. These are questions that will gather data not just to qualify the customer but also to authentically see if we are capable of creating the value.

Here are a few examples of Research Questions.
- How is business?
- Tell us about your business model please?
- What type of set-up do we have here?
- Please describe your product and service?
- Which areas of your business are you looking at for us to support you with?

All these are idea questions and they are morphed on the assumption that this is an exploratory stage both by you and the customer.

These questions generally hover above and around what might be public knowledge as well as private information. This is a preamble to a possible dance, a probable synergy. These questions create the groundwork, a platform for us to step up and forward into the eventual collaboration we want to bring about with our customer.

R2-REFLECTIVE QUESTIONS

These are questions that dive into the past of your customers profile and business. These questions go into the deeper recesses of their minds into the realms of the Romantic and, maybe also their Reactive Brain. Yes, organizations, like individuals, also have a semblance of the three-layered brain. The Reasoning Brain of an organization is where its processes, projects and working policies live. In the Romantic Brain of an organization, live and thrive their success stories, visions, missions and espoused values. In the Reactive Brain of an organization lie their fears and their competitive spirits.

So by emphasizing the power of Reflective questioning, we the salespeople and hopeful solution providers take a pulse of their culture, fears and expectations. Reflective questions are sensitively handled just as a good doctor will carefully check your pulse or place a stethoscope on your chest.

The responses we're searching for when asking Reflective questions are rarely found in books of accounts, company flyers or on the internet. The responses we are looking for are found in serendipitous moments, instances that unearth valuable, hidden information about hopes, fears and eventually, about growth.

Some examples of Reflective questions can be:
- Tell us about your past experiences with a supplier such as ourselves.
- Tell us how your previous product / processes / policies were successful.
- Might you have any ideas of how this whole need for this challenge came about?
- What exactly made your business grow so exponentially over the last decade?
- In the past, what exactly did you do that benefitted you?

the HeART of the CLOSE

The real idea behind Reflective questioning is for us to go into the past and discover potential, unearth strengths and find building blocks to create a powerful future.

R3-RESOURCE ASSESSMENT QUESTIONS

In old-school selling principles these questions would be termed qualifying questions. In the old-school language these would be assessing the buyer's capability of buying what we sell. Here in **the HeART of the CLOSE**, these questions are an authentic assessment of how much value can be created between us, the service provider and the customer.

Resource Assessment Questions are not just about whether they have the money but about whether they can truly afford what they are investing in. These questions are about finding out if the solution brought up in the conversation is, and will continue to be, a proper fit. These questions are about understanding the direct value and the potential side-effects of filling customer needs.

Resource Assessment Questions generate responses towards the reason, the rationality and the relevance of the purchase being considered. These questions are similar to the questions asked by a good doctor about diet preferences, allergies, current medications and potential side-effects of prescriptions being considered for a patient's needs.

Examples of Resource Assessment Questions are:
- When were you planning on making this investment?
- How much time would your team need to assess the benefits of our proposal?

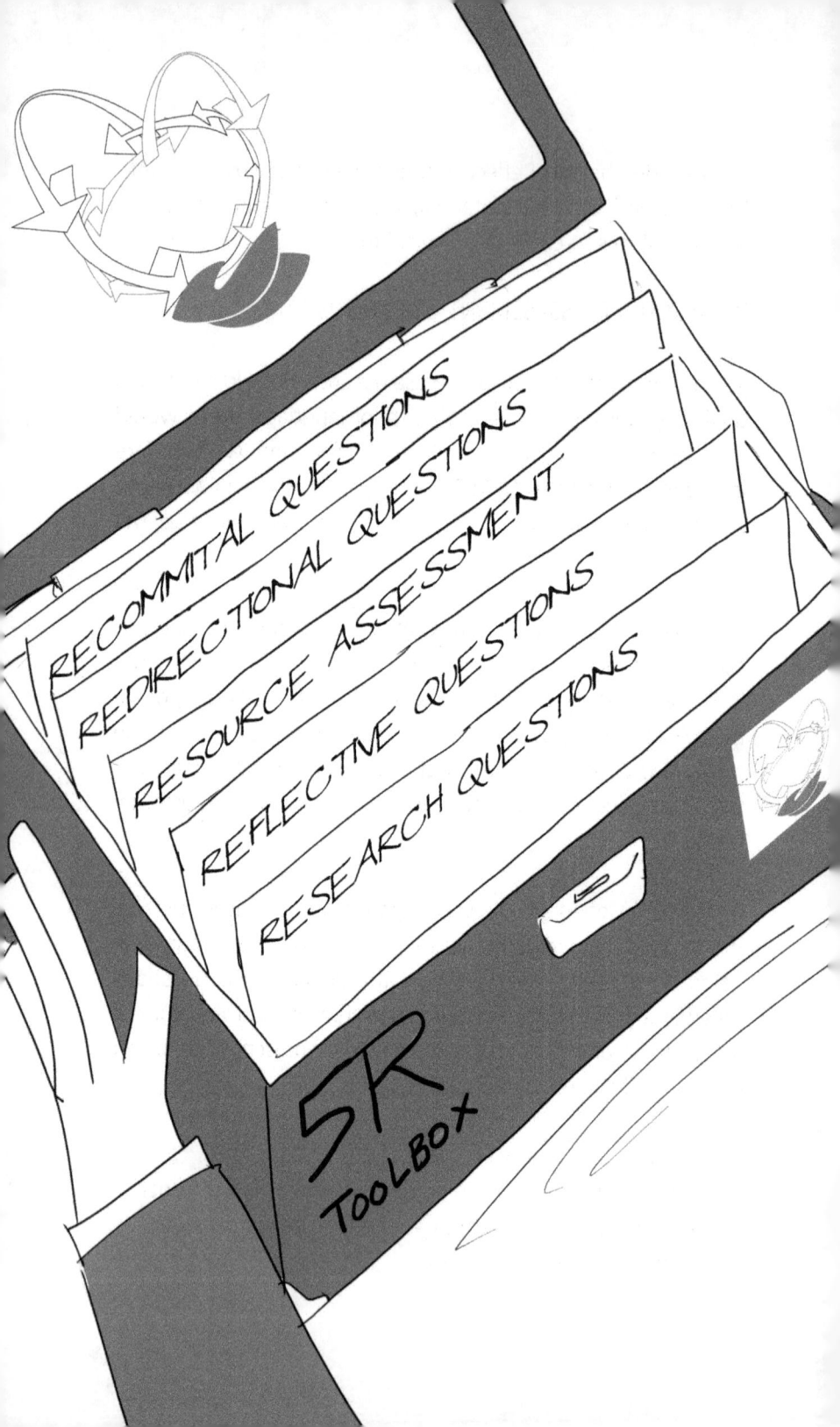

- What other information or tests do you need to make this purchase?
- Has your team tried products similar to ours before?

A few words of caution about this stage in the sales process and about questions in general – we, salespeople, must always start with beliefs for potential and possibilities in all sales interactions. We must then progress to verifying and validating intrinsically and tactfully. If we express doubt, have a demeanour of uncertainty and jump to conclusions about diversity, it can break the relationship and result in lost opportunities. We will, in the next few paragraphs, talk at length about this aspect, about how all questioning and inquiry processes have underlying assumptions and about how these assumptions can make or break co-creation.

R4-REDIRECTIONAL QUESTIONS

In Redirectional Questioning, we predominantly work with and convert the Romantic Brain more than the two other brains. Research questions work with the Reasoning Brain while reflective questioning about experiences, memories and feelings talks to the Romantic and the Reactive brain in tandem.

In the process of redirectional questioning we help the Romantic Brain visualize progress, growth and success arising directly from our recommended products or solutions. It is all about imagining increased profitability and a brighter future for the company.

Such visioning process is just as important in sales as it is in transformative change. With redirectional questioning your client begins to crystallize the thought in his mind, of employing of your products and services. In this process of visioning and future pacing, the Reasoning Brain takes a back-seat and the Romantic Brain and the Reactive Brain begin to buy into the idea with passion and intensity. Examples of redirectional questions:

- How does this whole solution package fit into your overall business strategy?
- What kind of impact do you foresee on company profits after deployment of this technology?
- Can you describe how your team will feel using this machinery, this process?

In traditional selling techniques of the past, this is the stage where the salesperson begins to exercise closing techniques. In **the HeART of the CLOSE**, we eliminate quick, hard-sell techniques and replace them with scientifically relevant methods that highlight ethical intentions and authentic concern. In **the HeART of the CLOSE**, we facilitate buying as a process of collaborating for growth and co-creating a future. The buyer then moves in to invest naturally, wilfully and fruitfully.

R5-RECOMMITTAL QUESTIONS

If we understood and apply the first four levels of questioning, then this last level may not even be necessary. In the first four levels, you placed the needs of the buyer before your own, researched well to understand them, reflected upon successes and hopes, made an assessment of resources and possibilities and, redirected their focus into the future.

In all the four previous stages, you have circled in and out of the reasons and realities of the three brains. At this stage, the

the HeART of the CLOSE

client has whole-heartedly set his mind on working with you and investing in your recommended solutions. Well, you did not actually "recommend" but had subtly and subconsciously implied some interventions for growth and profits for your customer.

The Recommital Questions summarize the previous discussions to integrate the assessments, the ideas to fill in possible loopholes in the diagnosis, and the still-to-be-discussed prescriptions. The Recommittal Questions confirm the discussion points and the highlights of the earlier conversations. Examples of Recommittal Questions are:

- Is it okay if we write up the points discussed?
- Correct me if I'm wrong. I understand you are ready to go ahead with this purchase next week?
- In your words, how does this whole prospect of improving your processes sound to you?
- It does seem like we'll have a lot of work to do together, right?
- Please do confirm that your team will be drawing out the paperwork on this arrangement.

Exercising the use of Recommittal Questions is like seating down all of the brains and getting consensus to the purchase being made. This is how you get them to say, "Yes!" in unison.

Again, if you have been diligent with the process of researching, reflecting, assessing resources and redirecting focus then this fifth stage of Recommittal Questions may not be necessary. Still, it is prudent to go through this stage because individual and organizational minds can and do change. This last stage is the process of launching your ship into the seas of progress.

Now, here's a deal on this process of inquiry, and it is in the form of a question. How does one go about choosing, morphing, sequencing and asking these questions?

That is a really good question, but before this book offers the answer, let's have a story.

In the movie, Finding Forrester, based on a book by James W. Ellison, William Forrester is a successful author of a literary piece of work called Avalon Landing. The success of Avalon Landing brings him a lot of media attention. Shy by nature, he turns inwards away from the limelight. He begins living the life of a recluse, holed up in a tiny apartment in Bronx, New York. There he spends his time reading, writing, reflecting, and washing his windows. While doing these, Mr. Forrester would get entranced every now and then by a game of basketball played on the neighbourhood streets by African-American kids.

One day, the ball they were playing with landed in his room through an open window. One of the boys came up to get the ball. The boy, Jamal, hailed from a simple family but had been lucky to get a scholarship in good school. As he walked away after retrieving the basketball from William Forrester, he happened to forget his little backpack by the author's door.

Hours later, the author noticed the backpack and as he carried it in, a large bunch of handwritten notes fell out from it. Out of curiosity, William Forrester began to read. He found the essays engrossing and unconsciously began to scribble comments and editorial notes on the papers. The next day Jamal picked up his bag and noticed the comments and suggestions by the recluse author. Soon the simple but talented boy and the ageing author became good friends, spending time in the author's apartment,

the HeART of the CLOSE

All filters are important and useful but none of them is as crucially sensitive as the filter of our personal biases and habits of pre-judging others.

talking and writing about school and life.

One day, over a cup of soup Jamal asks the author for the recipe so he could prepare the same soup for his mother and brother. Forrester happily shares the secret recipe with the young boy.

Weeks later, while discussing Jamal's writing submissions at school the African- American boy asked the author, "Say, how come you live alone up here and have no wife or anyone else?" This infuriated Forrester and in a rage he told Jamal to get out. An apologetic Jamal voiced his surprise and confusion. "Why does it upset you? What is the issue? Man, all I asked is how come you live alone and have no wife?"

Forrester cooled down and responded, "A few weeks ago you asked me how to make a good cup of soup and that was a good question. It was a question that had a purpose, preparing soup for your mother. Your question today serves no purpose other than being intrusive." Jamal, realized his error and stayed silent upon hearing the truth.

Likewise, in all business interactions, every time we form a question we must first run it through the filters of our own mind. We must ask ourselves the same questions Socrates

the HeART of the CLOSE

asked of his friend and let our inquiry have empowering and useful purposes.

Questions like:
- Will the question bring out useful facts?
- Will the question draw answers that benefit my customer?
- Will the question evoke answers that will help me help the client?
- Will the question take our business and partnership further?
- Are the questions well thought out, will they draw answers that stir up new thought and actions?

And the most important question we need to ask ourselves before articulating our inquiries is:
- Are we making any unqualified, unverified assumptions about our client's mindset, his intentions and his character?

Running your questions through your mind prior to voicing them out will filter and clarify your intentions and result in strong, purpose-driven questions like Jamal's soup question.

All filters are important and useful but none of them is as crucially sensitive as the filter of our personal biases and habits of pre-judging others. And we are often blind to our warped biases about people and cultures different from our own.

We cannot totally do away with assessing and judging others because it is part of human survival mechanism. We can, however, learn to be sensitive and aware of the lens we are looking through. Dr. Peter Senge, author and organizational consultant, claims, "The Eye Cannot See the Eye." And so we must constantly strive to clear our visions and our lenses.

FIVE: ULTIMATE TRUST IN ACTION AND ITS MEASURABILITY

I have highlighted the power of action when it comes to success and I'd like to also reinforce it when it comes to successes in our conversations.

My school, the Sardar Dastur Hoshang Boys High School left major impressions in me about kindness, respect for others and personal presence. The immortal words "Humata, Hukata" were encrypted on our school badges. It is in a language unknown to me but was kindly translated by the teachers. It means "Good Thoughts, Good Words."

I was in my pre-teens and like most of the boys in school, I assumed it meant we must do away with foul language and vulgarity in our daily conversations and interactions. Not until I reached my 20s did I go back and ponder upon the depths, the simplicity and the precision of the philosophy embedded in those two words – Humata, Hukata. Upon further research today, I learned that there is a third and more powerful word to complete that immortal affirmation phrase. That word is Hvrashta and the full motto is Humata, Hukata, and Hvrashta. Translated, it means, "Good Thoughts, Good Words and Good Deeds."

Come to think of it, how many times in our lives do we brim with and demonstrate good intentions? No I don't just mean the random thoughts of kindness flashing through our minds but also the love, the compassion and the desire to create filling our conscious and unconscious thoughts. It is in our human nature to be made up of these feelings of kindness, compassion and the desire to grow and create the value.

the HeART of the CLOSE

These thoughts and feelings exist in all individuals. But how frequently does the world around us come to know about what individuals think and feel? How many times does the world read our mind and understand our hearts? The good thoughts in our minds and hearts, or Humata, stay hidden. They lie undiscovered until they take some form of expression.

We can convert emotions and ideas into words, into pitches and presentations for the good we want to contribute to the world, for the value creation we want to bring to our markets, thus raising creativity and innovation to the next level. Hukata -good words or empowering expressions can be seen, heard and felt. They are at a higher level more tangible than good thoughts, ideas and emotions. And yet, words and empowering expressions that claim competence, offer solutions and promise growth and innovation are rendered cheap and useless unless they can be converted into action, into something tangible which can be measured and accounted for. Words can inspire hope and draw applause but it is real positive action, Hvrashta, that fills the stomachs of armies and builds the bridges that take us where we want to go and grow. The pillars that measure success, growth and self-fulfilment are rooted in action.

That word is Hvrashta and the full motto is Humata, Hukata, and Hvrashta. Translated, it means, "Good Thoughts, Good Words and Good Deeds."

Action and the execution of plans and goals are paramount both to improving business profitability and to achieving real results in personal development. Action is where the rubber meets the road and where customer traction is acquired and gained.

Action is of two kinds. The first kind is action taken within the mind such as holding back our impatience, holding back our impulses and managing our anger. These internal "actions" are sometimes referred to as emotional intelligence. The other kind of action is where you roll up your sleeves, pick up the phone and call a hundred potential customers in a day. The power lies in the doing. It is in taking this action repeatedly, day after day, that the proverbial Mountain begins to roll towards Mohammad.

Sales and the discipline of selling is a numbers game. It is about persistence and perspiration. It is about taking one rejection after another.

The ability to hold back anxiety, the fortitude to face repeated failure is laudable internal action that is sensed and felt, but it is unmeasurable and not visible. Getting up and getting out of your comfort zone day after day is action that is physical, external, and visible. It is seen and felt by others. Both types of actions must be performed often and with undiminishing energy so as to grow, obtain results, and achieve massive success. This is what moves mountains and creates change. When the mountains move, you, the salesperson, can then take a measuring tape and record your success, counting the times you walk into your bank with the fruit of success.

I know of a small family business many years ago, run by a newlywed couple in Miami Florida where English and Spanish were spoken because of the large number of Latin American residents. This couple wanted to become a major supplier of children's wear to the Wal-Mart chain of stores in the US.

They had a lot of passion and energy but not much industry knowledge and even less local language and culture.

They figured out three ways to grow. Firstly, find a large number of good suppliers from the other parts of the world; secondly, know the business and build a good operations and management team; and thirdly, master the local language and culture to maximize opportunities to grow their organization. They decided to build relationships with at least one new external supplier of children's wear every year. They decided to learn 20 new Spanish words a week between them so they could communicate better with their managers, workers and local partners. Before the arrival of the internet and Google this was not an easy task, but they kept to their attainable and actionable growth milestones without hindering their daily routines. In less than two years of working on these goals, their business moved up from 2 million dollars a year to 15 million dollars a year. They soon became one of the top suppliers of Wal-Mart and they' had dug their roots into a new culture and a new country. Now, decades later, nearly 10% of the children's wear on the shelves of Wal-Mart stores across the US come from their company in Florida. Action, they say, speaks louder than words. It is action that nourishes your health, happiness and wealth.

With the end of this chapter, we conclude the fundamentals required to be successful in sales and in other conversations toward the pursuit of progress and growth in life. In the ensuing chapters, we will constantly draw upon these five ideals.
- Clarify intentions and objectives.
- Enhance sensory awareness and presence of mind through the following:
  - Find quiet ground

- Manage state of mind
- Listen well
- Recognize diverse points of view and adapt to changing circumstances.
- Develop an eagerness to learn so as to innovate and grow constantly.
- Trust action and its measurability.

These five fundamentals of powerful and developmental interactions are not just good for selling and other communicative skill sets but also very applicable to all things progressive in life-intent, awareness, respect for diversity, curiosity to learn and the ability to take action through all endeavours and challenges.

CHAPTER 4

THE HEART OF THE SALES PROCESS

Selling is a process, and the stages of this process can be nebulous. It takes a while to understand and master the process, and the stages differ from industry to industry. These stages also continuously change over time as trends, technology and theories of business evolve. In the 1950s, transactional selling was the trend. Sales professionals drew attention to their products and services, generated the desire to buy in the buyer's mind and then moved in to close the deal. The process was salesperson driven and was typically a one-way street called Push.

In the 80s when the range of products and services began to grow and the roads to market became congested, companies employed efforts to sell their products and services based on improved features, better advantages and increased benefits for the customer. The traffic in the business of selling was still jam-packed as during the Push streets, but the sales process was turning more tactical and smarter.

By the 1990s and into the new millennium, the world had had enough of being a material world and the trends became a lot more strategic and ecological. Sales professionals began learning to walk in their customer's shoes. They began to think in terms of providing long-term ecological and sustainable solutions for their customers. The selling world began to realize that the hit-and-run techniques of the past weren't working and did not make business sense or monetary logic. At the turn of the century and deep into the second decade of the 21st century, the profession of selling and the business it represented began to think in terms of the big picture, in systems and interconnectivity. The business world and the selling profession realized the power and the wisdom of being altruistic, eco-conscious, value creators in the world.

This does not, at all, mean profits and profit making have been put aside. It means people have realized the long-term sense of nurturing and sustaining the resources from planet Earth. They have realized that all people are inter-connected. Exploiting and taking advantage of one group of people eventually harms many others and affects the entire world. Business and professional salespeople have realized that making better use of the Earth's resources and treating people fairly makes mighty good business sense. This is how smart businesses reap huge profits year after year.

The HeART of the CLOSE is about closing more deals but especially, about coming from the heart. It's about being ethical in approach, conscientious in analysis and creative in proving value-creating solutions. Above all, it's about making sure the interventions provided do no systemic harm to the consumer, to the company, and to the ecology. Thus, it is not about greedily

the HeART of the CLOSE

closing deals in the old way but about diligently diagnosing needs, offering options, earning trust and establishing long-term partnerships with the client/customer. This book is also about getting the brains–the Reasoning Brain, the Romantic Brain and the Reactive Brain– in alignment towards the solution and value creation.

From an organizational and corporate perspective, the Reasoning Brain represents the analytical business side of the company, the Romantic Brain represents the visionary aspirations of the company and the Reactive Brain represents its values and deep-rooted culture. These three aspects of an organization need to come into an alignment for the company to grow, flourish, and lead in its field.

I must also highlight the rapid growth of communication technology, the internet and the influence of social media in the last two decades. Because of this, the selling profession has had to adjust its stance, change garb, and fly rapidly to keep up with the explosive growth of information disbursement that has become part and parcel of the world we live in today.

The essential soft skills and people skills that produce successful sales personnel have not changed much but now, these skills need to adapt and wrap themselves around new technology, new resources and new challenges. In *the HeART of the CLOSE*, I have made efforts to touch upon and run parallel to this baseline of information disbursement. I also urge the professional salesperson of today to equip himself to face evolving trends and changing technology.

THE BUYER SIDE HEART

One disclaimer before I start talking about how individuals and companies discover their needs and wants and then move into filling those needs and wants. I want to leave out a very special group of buyers. My apologies, but I have been unable to wrap my Indian turban around the idea why some people, when they see large red signs announcing "a Sale," drop everything they are doing and dash to out buy everyone and purchase everything in sight. It is a phenomenon I want to leave untouched and unexplored in this book. Ha ha!

How does the rest of the world go about buying? How do they come to the conclusion that they need something and what steps do they take to fill those needs? And just to differentiate ever so slightly between a need and a want, let me just say this. A need is a highly cerebral, highly thought-through gap that may be of a material thing or a service. Needs are mostly functional and our Reasoning Brain is usually in full approval of that need or gap, but the Reasoning Brain needs to get consensus from the Romantic and the Reactive Brain before needs get filled. A want, on the other hand, is more of a form or fantasy versus function, and wants occur more from our Romantic Brain and Reactive Brain.

For example, if our workplace is far from our homes, we realize the wisdom of investing in an automobile to save time, effort, and cost. This is categorized as a need. But if it makes more sense to travel to a distant workplace on a public utility bus or train, and yet we want to invest in a two-seater, red Maserati convertible with an über cool sound system, this is categorized as a want. I am obviously over simplifying and exaggerating between a need and a want but I think you get the picture.

the HeART of the CLOSE

Stages of the Buyer Side Heart

Potential buyers go through five stages of the sales process.

Stage ONE: REALIZES AND FOCUSES ON NEEDS

In the above example, the first stage is when they first come to a conclusion that there is a need to buy an automobile for transportation. The moment this realization crystallizes, our potential customers simultaneously look around and assess what is available in the marketplace. This looking around is simultaneous to realizing the need because in today's internet-driven world, data and information are available to customers with just a few taps on their computers.

Stage TWO: CANVASSES AND EVALUATES OPTIONS

At stage 2, our potential customers go through a process of refining preferences and narrowing down possibilities based on availability, budget and other relevant criteria. This is the stage for comparing features, advantages and benefits. The work done in this stage is mostly by the Reasoning brain with some support by the Romantic and the Reactive Brain. It is also possible that the latter two brains become a little more involved and excited over a specific product. To an experienced salesperson, that is a buying signal and yet, a good salesperson stays on the outskirts of this stage's comparison process by the buyer. That is good practice because in stage 2, the buyer is working on achieving clarity of her own needs within her own mind. It is wise on the part of the salesperson to offer information, support the analysis being done by the buyer, and wait until the buyer invites the salesperson in to participate in this process.

the HeART of the CLOSE

Stage THREE: IDENTIFIES SOLUTIONS, MAKES A CHOICE

As the buyer works through the ocean of options and available information, greater clarity is eventually achieved by him. Here, the dialogue becomes consensual among the three brains of the buyer and results in eventual alignment towards a single choice, a solution that fits the need gap realized during the first stage of the buying process. These first three stages vary in duration and complexity depending on the size and the complexity of the need gap. It also differs across multiple industries and businesses. The experienced salesperson is well-versed in this area. He knows how much information to offer, when to intervene and how much patience and persistence are required.

My personal experience in the area of juggling the right mix of patience and persistence came about from the days I had sold large-scale air conditioning projects; investment in the future's commodities markets and large-scale consumer goods for department stores. I gained mastery over this deliberate process and the nuances of working with colleagues and partners in the apparel district of New York, USA. The journey to mastery came with many challenges before the exhilarating realization. I remember a spring day after I had booked myself solid for the next two seasons. Sitting in my office, I looked out the window and a quiet serenity engulfed me. It struck me how simple closing new business becomes once you acquire industry knowhow and learn to patiently wait for your buyers to think and decide in your favor.

It's like stumbling and swaying as you learn to ride a bicycle. You remember that feeling? After days of struggle and trepidation, after several bruised knees and elbows, you finally get it. You finally know how to get started, where to look, how tightly to hold the handles and how much pedalling is needed to acquire balance and momentum. The resulting feeling is exhilarating. It's like the cool breeze running through you as you coast downhill on an open road. Achieving mastery in selling is a bit like that.

Stage FOUR: NEGOTIATES, MAKES THE PURCHASE

The next stage on the buyer's side perspective is when the buyer needs to put ideas together after she identifies the solution that will fill her need gap. During my college workshop days while studying engineering, we used to die, mould and cast simple machine parts. The process of a buyer acquiring a chosen solution for her needs can be likened to moulding, casting, finishing and fitting a square peg into a square hole. Even when we have correctly measured and cut a square peg to fit a square hole, the process of coupling or fitting things takes a bit of work. It is a dance of negotiation that needs a little twist, a turn and sometimes a little grease. Here, I absolutely do not mean the use of the word "grease" in its negative sense. I refer to "grease" as the sensitivity and care needed to arrive at a perfect alignment.

At this stage when the buyer takes in and acquires the solutions for her need (a square peg for a square hole) adjustments and negotiations still need to be done as a necessary part of the purchasing cycle. It is necessary to get the smoothest possible fit in terms of size, specifications, quality, time, money and continued support and service for the products we sell. In the second part of this chapter, we will talk about the nuances of negotiating effectively and fruitfully while looking at the process from the salesperson's perspective,

the HeART of the CLOSE

Stage FIVE: UTILIZES THE SERVICES AND PROVIDES FEEDBACK

The last stage for the buyer's side heart is the process of using and enjoying the newly acquired product or service. In today's eco-conscious and ethical culture of doing business, this 5th stage, is as important as the 4 other stages of buying. If we, as salespeople, have been diligent and have provided a valuable product and service, then the buyer becomes our endorser for life and we become her partner. This is the path to service and sustainability over long periods of time.

THE SELLER SIDE HEART

Across industries, a typical sales cycle can have five, seven or even nine stages to it. Some of the stages are still included only because of the old ways of transaction selling or the pushing kind of selling. **The HeART of the CLOSE** takes into account that today, ethics, eco-consciousness and value creation are key factors to be considered in all businesses.

Before we take up the stages at the seller side, I would like to introduce two extremely important concepts about ethics, eco-consciousness and value creation, represented by these words.

Congruence

Let us first look at the concept and the word "congruence" in both communication and behaviour. What does this mean? What does it represent? Why is it important and what can be done about it?

In the presence of other people most of us almost always have two ongoing conversations–our internal conversation and the external exchange. These two conversations are most always tri-model; we use words, images and kinaesthesia when speaking with ourselves internally and when speaking with others externally. For the moment let's switch the word kinaesthesia to "feelings." Thus we are almost always communicating within and outside of us in words, images and feelings. You can also say we are almost always communicating internally and externally in language, gestures and other auditory non-verbals like tonality, pitch of voice, etc.

Congruence in communication is when our conversations with ourselves and our conversations with others are in harmony. When they have reached maximum alignment and consensus then we can claim that we have achieved congruence. A simplistic example of a lack of congruence is when I say I am feeling confident but inside of me, I'm telling myself, "Hey that is such a big lie! I am scared to bits." In that moment, we are out of congruence. This simplistic example is just a state of mind description. Think of when you are completely out of the sync with your spouse's beliefs and values but on the outside, you carry on an exhibiting that you are. Consider how much discord your words create inside you and in your interactions with your spouse.

Thus, congruence can be synonymous to being aligned, authentic, truthful, in the flow. It is all of that but much, much more. Taking up the analogy

> Congruence can be synonymous to being aligned, authentic, truthful, in the flow. It is all of that but much, much more.

of the Reasoning, the Romantic and the Reactive Brain it can be said, only when the conversations among these three are in harmony and in tune that congruence arises.

In life and in the selling business, competent salespeople and perceptive buyers can see, hear and feel this. When your customers see this lack of congruence in the salesperson there is no way they will put their trust in you. No way will you be able to build rapport. No way will you get to move together to the synergistic dance of mutual value creation. The absence of internal alignment leads to a non-existent external alignment in partnership.

I could quickly list down a few bullet points to answer the question in your mind about what you can do to achieve congruence, but that would be taking a shortcut and providing your curiosity a temporary, superficial relief rather than giving you a permanent, long-lasting cure. Work with me through the whole process, through all the principles and the practices of **the HeART of The CLOSE** and you will have learned how to fish and feed yourself success in sales, in business and in life.

Now, let's say for the meantime you have mastered the ability to consistently achieve congruence. Let's say you have become proficient at coupling together your intentions and actions towards achieving desired outcomes. Let us say you are now a virtuoso at creating harmony between your conscious and sub-conscious thinking. Let's just say that your Reasoning, Romantic and Reactive Brains know how to rock and roll well together. Not only do you know how to rock and roll on your own inside your own mind but you also have acquired uncanny abilities to nudge the minds of others to rock and roll to the beat of your music. You have become the king of connecting with, engaging

and influencing others. You are unstoppable and you can sell anything to anyone, anytime you want. If you wanted to and if the world permitted it, you could sell shiploads of snow to Eskimos.

Now here is where the second concept, ecology, kicks in. It's when you ask yourself if selling snow to Eskimos is the right thing to do, even when you know they are hungering for snow and you can close that kind of a deal anytime.

Ecology

Ecology is becoming conscientious of the big-picture outcomes that we create with ourselves, with our teams and in partnership with our customers. Ecology is when we think big-picture and consider the long-term and systemic effects of our selling interventions. Ecology is when we take into account the ripple effects of our conversations and creations in selling and development. Ecology is thinking compassion, thinking benign. It's considering first the planet, then the people and finally, profits. Ecological thinking is systems thinking in action.

Dr. Peter Senge, author of the Fifth Discipline, once shared with me a story about Nike. When it was in the pinnacle of success, Nike was investing time and effort in researching and developing 100% biodegradable shoes. Even now in 2015, shoes use synthetic glue, metal rivets and other stuff. Think of the remarkable positive ecological impact if even the rivets and the glue can turn to dust.

In selling, we cater not just to the needs but also to the wants of the Romantic and the Reactive Brain of our customers. We cater to their emotions and aspirations, and so it becomes our

responsibility to ensure we leave no scars on their emotions and spirits. That is ecology.

This book liberally and interchangeably uses the words prospect, buyer, client and customer but the concept of ecology applies to all. It means every one we deal with must be regarded as human beings like ourselves, just as we regard ourselves as persons like them, made out of memories, spirit, emotions, and relationships.

To wrap up, congruence is the concept of finding, creating and sustaining alignment in our internal beliefs and thoughts with our external words and actions. Ecology is working in alignment with the beliefs, values, emotions, and material needs of other people and the larger system.

We have covered sufficient ground to understand the underlying principles leading to powerful interactions in sales and in life. In the succeeding paragraphs, the book will cover the five stages to **The HeART of the CLOSE**. As earlier mentioned there is a process to selling—**the HeART of the CLOSE**—and the cycle time of this process varies across products and industries. At a retail sales point the cycle time may take two minutes whereas in selling, say, large-scale air conditioning plant projects the cycle time could take two months or longer.

Regardless of the length of time according to different industries, a typical sales cycle or process goes through these five, chunk sized stages: connect, engage, influence, acquire and serve.

A two-minute sales cycle at a breakfast fast food place might start with "Good morning! Welcome to McDonalds" and end with "Thank you, come again!"

A sales cycle in a project engineering company takes months and could go through introduction, initial presentation, qualifying conversation, diagnostics, proposals 1, 2, 3, followed by more presentations, clarifications, negotiations, etc.

What is important in both, the two-minute cycle and the two-month cycle is a salesperson consciously knows at all times which stage of the sales process she is in. Any hastiness, restlessness, over-eagerness or laggardness may disrupt the process and derail the business opportunity.

Let's now work through the nuances and requirements of each stage so we, salespeople, can maintain awareness of the process at all times. We can then avoid jumping ahead, lagging behind, or sleep walking through a stage and consequently, losing the business.

Stages of the Seller Side Heart

Stage ONE: CONNECT WITH CLARITY

In Chapter 1, you read about the old salesman's adage, "Always be prospecting." That, when viewed from today's technology-driven, constantly-wired, 24/7 world, becomes a moot point. Today, regardless of industry, profession or function, people are constantly on the move. Whether consciously or unconsciously, they are somehow always prospecting. Because we are constantly on the move and constantly working, we are often high-strung, running around helter-skelter, and pointlessly burning up our personal energy and the company resources. What we have to do is narrow our focus and smartly select the tasks and areas where we can fruitfully apply our energies and resources.

the HeART of the CLOSE

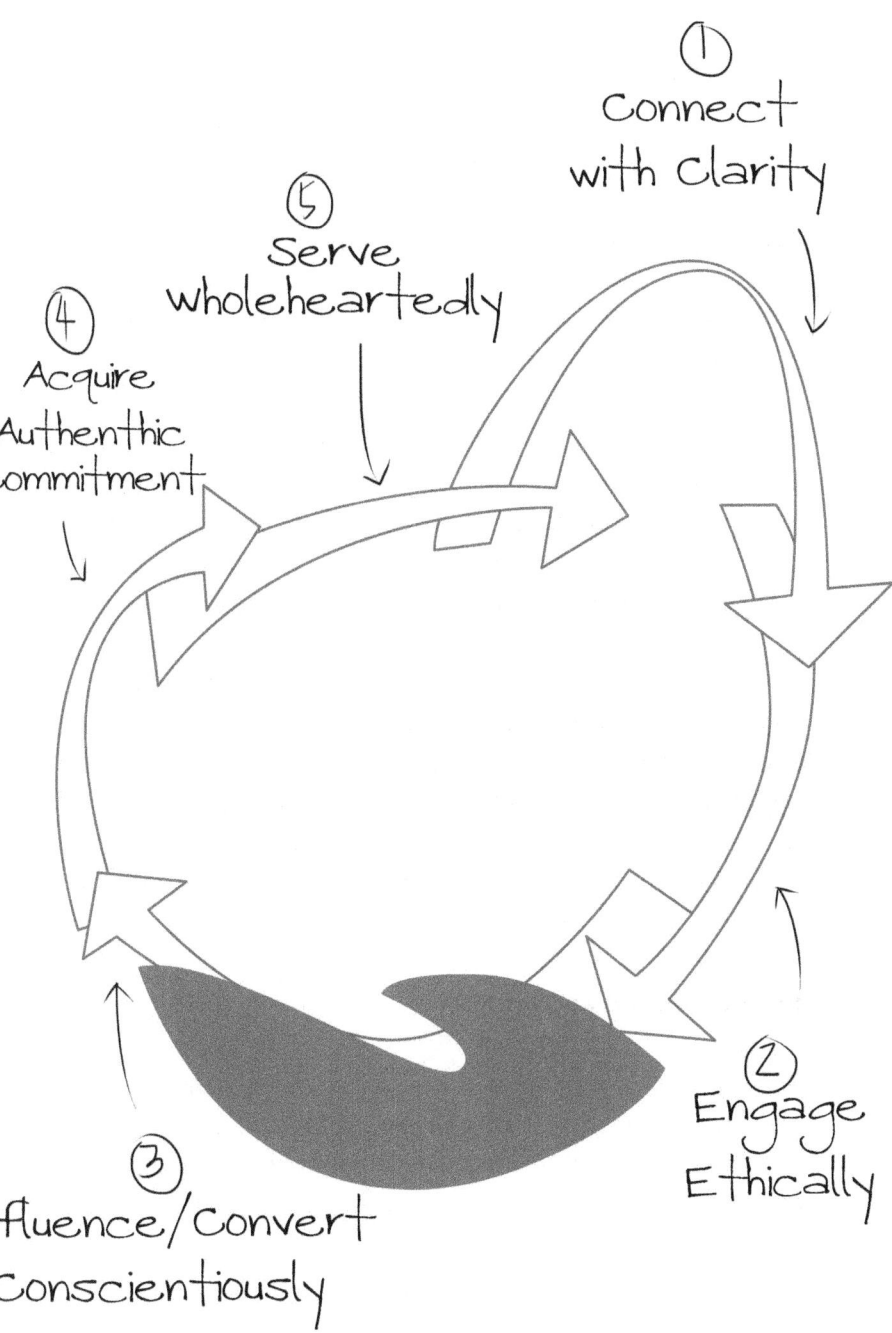

① Connect
with Clarity

⑤ Serve
wholeheartedly

④ Acquire
Authenthic
Commitment

③ Influence/Convert
Conscientiously

② Engage
Ethically

At the Connect with Clarity stage, it is crucial for the sales person to be totally conversant about factors that influence how buyers connect with products and services, namely:

Product Knowledge and Market Position

Many salespeople commit the serious mistake of trying to wing it and just sell the box, so to speak. The conscientious salesperson will take time and put effort into fully understanding her company's range of products, their functions and applications. She will also spend time and energy in familiarizing herself with other products similar to her own which are accessible to her potential customers. The more she knows about her product and other parallel products, the better her hand will be at selling.

It also works to her advantage if she knows about the industry and the market conditions in which the business strives and ebbs. A salesperson with an ear to the ground knows when opportunities are ripe and when to pluck and harvest. But a salesperson who sleeps on the job of knowing what is going on in the marketplace would inevitably be squeezed out of the race toward selling success.

Business Brand and Identity

A salesperson who wants to excel at selling, works hand in hand with the marketing department and the whole organization. She knows and is up to date with the history, reputation and goodwill that exist around the product or service she represents.

The product's reputation and the company's goodwill enhance the perception of a broader audience in the marketplace. This is the brand. Sometimes the perception and the product are a perfect match and sometimes they are not in tandem. Selling becomes easy if brand recognition precedes actual introduction of the product or service. But over time, leads coming solely from brand recognition do not sustain. Selling is challenging when a product's reputation has yet to be built. A salesperson with accurate knowledge knows the kind of efforts she needs to put in and is objective about the results of her efforts toward promoting the brand.

Personal Identity and Personal Branding

This one is big and I am in agreement with successful sales leaders who claim its importance. This is why sales coaches recommend a salesperson first sell herself before she begins to sell the product or the service she represents.

It is important for us to have a good assessment of our own beliefs, values and skills. Selling and buying are a matter of gaining and giving trust rather than just a transaction of tangibles and non-tangibles. I have, many times, come across salespeople who do not have a clear picture of who they are and what their own needs and value points are. Our values and beliefs form our personalities and these values and beliefs need to have a certain cohesion and harmony with what we profess, promote or sell.

Our buyers and clients continually assess us. When they see, hear and sense our own faith and confidence in our products and services, their faith and confidence in those products and services increase.

Many years ago, I received a cold call from an insurance agent of Indian origin in the Philippines. I agreed to an appointment as

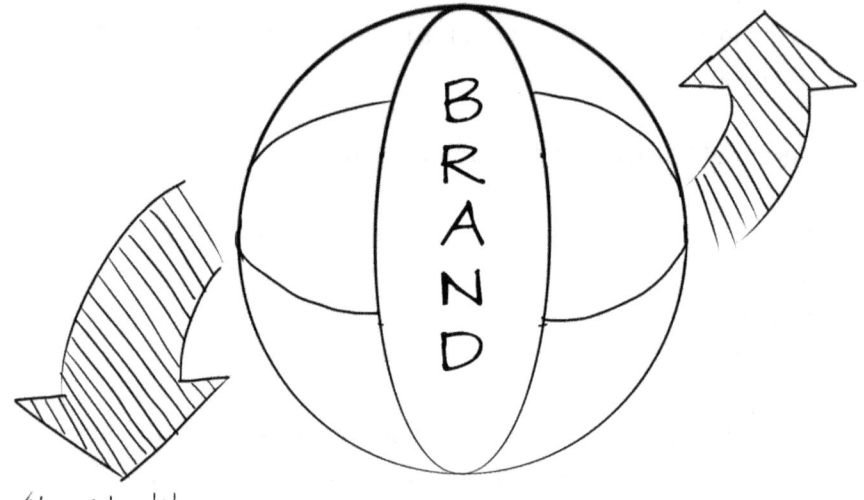

√Their Perception
√Their Benefits
√Their Impression
√Their Song & Delight
√Their Growth

√Your Identity
√Your Creation
√Your Value Proposition
√Your Theme & Campaign
√Your Service

respectful consideration of our common ethnic background and because he represented a reputable company in the Philippines, plus I did have a need for life insurance at that time in my life. I asked him to fax me the proposal a few days ahead of our appointment and to phone me one more time after I receive the proposal before coming over to my office to see me. Days passed. I did not receive any proposal by fax and neither did I receive another phone call.

An hour after the agreed time and date of the appointment this insurance salesperson turned up at my office accompanied by his wife, who was dressed to the hilt. She looked as if she were going to a party rather than a business meeting. Out of courtesy, I put aside my work at hand and gave them my attention and time. His pitch didn't go beyond the fact that investing in life insurance was important and he represented a highly reputable firm in the Philippines. I, technically, wasn't just a hot lead but a serious prospect and he was jumping the gun as far as the process and even etiquette were concerned. I needed details and assurance before I made a decision and before his attempts to close.

I actually wanted to buy and I thought I'd help him educate and convince me but my questioning and probing wasn't getting us anywhere. Finally, out of desperation, I asked, "So tell me, have you and your wife invested in any of the products offered by your company?"

Sad to say the answer was a "No" from both of them. Although I actually needed insurance and the product and service they represented might have been good, I had to ease them out of my office and out of my life because of the sheer absence of professionalism and common courtesy from this salesperson.

A conscientious salesperson must know the product and must have faith and confidence in the product, the organization and the industry. And it must manifest in his behaviour and in his professionalism when touching base with prospects.

Prospect Profusely and Professionally
Initiate Dialogue

It is not common for potential customers to be as accommodating and accessible as I was for this insurance salesperson of Indian origin in the Philippines. To find potential customers to connect with, we need to prospect, and we need to do it profusely and professionally.

Many years ago I heard this story about a shoe salesman who was sent to a remote, unexplored island country to look for business. He came back to his manager after a short while, claiming the people of that island country were uncivilized and backward. They wore no shoes, no footwear at all! He concluded the island country wasn't a potential market for their products.

The manager o the shoe company then sent another salesperson to the same remote, uncivilized, backward island country. She came back a few quick days later all excited and happy and declared to the manager that the island country was the biggest possible marketplace because the people had no shoes at all! It was an opportunity of a lifetime for their company.

The story is about a salesperson's mindset but it also puts across a point. We, in marketing and sales, must first, seek constantly to expand and increase our range. Secondly, we need to be selective about how and where we put our energies, our time and our resources.

To prospect profusely and effectively, we must include the elements of precision and discipline into our prospecting activities. Numerous ways of prospecting abound, which vary depending on the kind of business you represent. Prospecting

for retail business is a totally different animal compared to prospecting for business-to-business selling projects. Our focus here, in **The HeART of The CLOSE**, is on business-to-business selling or, at least not off-the-counter selling.

Five keys to improving efficiency and focus in prospecting.

a. The Right Marketplace

Keeping in mind the story of the shoe salesperson in a remote island, consider these three things. First, what exactly do you want to sell and how much distance from your selling point do you want to reach? Whatever is reasonable and feasible for you and your company is your geographical area. Within this geographical area, you need to find the location of the highest concentration in numbers of your target clients.

Secondly, within the chosen geographical area with a high concentration of your target clients, you need to narrow down your focus on their psyche. Research on what they like. What turns them off, what fulfils their buying needs, and what fulfils their business-and-living needs? What are their life and social habits? What are the kinds of terrain, weather and living conditions surrounding them which influence their life and social habits?

whatever is reasonable and feasible for you and your company is your geographical area.

Thirdly, what are their economic and financial conditions? How much money do they have or want to spend for your kind

the HeART of the CLOSE

of products and services. Is this level of social and financial status right for them–condominiums by the beach that your company sells?

Surely, all these data can be acquired through market research companies and your marketing department will provide these details, but you should also highlight what works for you and your personality.

b. The Authentic Approach

When you are knocking on doors selling and/or at the keyboard, meeting people through emails, chat-rooms, and social groups, learn to call a spade exactly that. I have been approached many times in person or through the internet with offers to change my life one way or another. I then figure out this is not the real intention of the person approaching me. It is best to state your purpose truthfully, directly and in the simplest way.

If you are an insurance agent, first find out if they'd be interested to hear what you have to offer. If you are a real estate agent, introduce yourself and ask your prospect if they are in the market to invest even if your source has pinpointed them to you as a high potential person. Never approach with the assumption that they are interested, even if all the research and referrals say so. Ask! Ask, seek information and then present yourself.

You must be clear and authentic when you touch base, one human being to another, although there certainly has to be some kind of an advertisement or draw. Creating the hype, buzz and noise is the job of your marketing department.

c. Provide Value at First Touch

Utilize your first contact to open up the conversation, to create value and leave a mark. You may want to share valuable information, a certain insight or a tip, anything about how they can resolve their business or personal challenges

While prospecting or gathering leads to websites or in e-mail marketing and over social network, many good marketers and salespeople leave a little gift such as a voucher, a discount coupon, or free registration. This part-marketing and part-selling on the internet is done because the conversation is usually not human-to-human nor in real-time and thus, producing a slight time gap. If we have real-time, face-to-face, chats online, I would emphasize more caution because firstly, not being physical present eliminates the aspects of kinaesthesia and feeling during conversations; and secondly, every single byte and pixel of the conversation can be recorded and traced back even when offline. Errors and omissions in such conversations are harder to forget or accept.

d. Multiple Modality Touches

We know the human brain is divided into the Rational, the Romantic and the Reactive Brains; we also know that this Triune Brain digests, stores, utilizes and articulates through the five senses. To increase the chances and facilitate the entry of new information so it gains acceptance from all three brains, it makes sense to mix these five modalities well and in good proportion.

If you are sending an introduction e-mail it is wise to include some relevant visuals. If you are sending images, it is a good idea to send an audio file with it. If you are making a phone call,

the HeART of the CLOSE

then send over pictures or charts beforehand so your potential customer can browse through them while you are chatting with them.

Really good communicators (a.k.a. super sales-persons) know how to assemble, change and morph their words. They utilize visual, auditory and tactile communication modalities accompanied by images or actual samples. They use picturesque, descriptive language. They share stories that show, more than tell.

e. Give Space and Keep it Open

Early on in the Connect with Clarity stage of a sales cycle, do not be over eager or excited and pushy. One adage good salespeople always follow is "do not create a need where none exists." Creating a need where none exists is like working the sales cycle up to build a skyscraper of expectations without really putting down the cornerstone foundation of strength and support.

Especially in the early stages—but also throughout the whole sales cycle—stay open to letting go and losing rather than pursuing pointlessly and suffering over the long term. Of course, knowing early on from a customer saves us time, effort and money.

An investment consultant friend of mine from Mumbai, India has devised an algorithm which correctly analyses the input effort to the outcome result of each stage of the sales cycle. He has figured out when the best time is to cut losses while chasing a new customer in his industry.

While practicing the keys for prospecting profusely, a well-planned, well-rehearsed pitch will lead our prospects into the next engagement level. Many good salespeople with good services fall out of the race because they did not put together a concise opening and introduction statement about themselves, their products and their company.

A simple and effective format to prepare and maintain a pitch is built in five steps. You may re-arrange the text a bit based on the touch point you are putting across, and you may add an opening greeting in a question format. Please refer to the 5R Questioning Toolbox in Chapter 3 for questioning powerfully.

The Five-step Format to Making a Pitch:

a. **Make an irrefutable claim about you and your company's services; about your own and your company's competencies and achievements. Claim it.**

Example: Our company, ISA Inc., is among the top ten training companies in the region and most of our developmental programs are action-research based.

b. **Highlight a need gap for the prospect. Creatively and gently articulate your customer's need and your product/service's ability to address it. Briskly describe how your service resolves business and personal challenges for the customers. Frequently use the words, "You", "Yours" and "To your benefit".**

Example: With this merger you will acquire 3,000 new employees and it will greatly benefit management to increase alignment and engagement with the mother company's goals. We can influence and create such a culture as we have done for 7 other multinationals in the past 5 years. These interventions improved

performance and productivity by 20% within 3 months. The same can happen for you.

c. **Share testimonies in story formats about how your product or service has helped your other customers. Do this quickly, in two or three sentences.**

Example: Without having to give new discounts and with less than 5% employee turnover, ABC Hotels reduced their cancellations by 20% in the last 5 quarters.

Highlight current-day benefits for the prospect. Mention how the same service, benefit and story are even more relevant in today's economy.

Example: Assuming hospitals like yours work like hotels, you can, with our support, optimize the use of your operating rooms, wards, corridors and even elevators. Imagine serving 20% more patients a year with your currently available resources.

d. **Give your prospect recommendations on what to do in an open, flowing way.**

Example: Consider letting us partner with your Learning Center and we can, together, create a 9-month Leadership and Communications curriculum tailored to your needs and business model.

e. **Offer a sample /demo piece or invite them for a viewing and free trial of your product or your work.**

Example: If it's alright with you, two of our consultants can come down here next week and present short, hypothetical scenarios with solutions relevant to the healthcare industry. Just give us a date and time.

Make sure your spiel and this whole pitch is quick, concise and open-ended. Your job here is to leave the prospects thinking and wanting to dig up more information.

Example: As I'm sure you already know, businesses are about improved internal processes and better customer service. The answer to both is to become a learning organization.

Remember, you are not presenting the whole nine yards and neither are you lunging mindlessly towards a close. Forget what the old-timers used to say about "always be closing." That is a past-century myth. Your purpose is value creation and this first step is to simply build a relationship with your prospect's Rational and Romantic Brain to open up space for dialogue.

You can, at this stage, pave success in the market if your prospect responds with a question or two and a desire to know more.

This little spiel or pitch you write up must be straightforward and easy to understand. It must be equally effective on e-mail and over the phone, with a few edits. It should not be more than a minute or a minute-and-a-half. It should get you traction while in an elevator or while waiting in line for a taxi. It should never exceed 150 words.

Stage TWO: ENGAGE CREATIVELY AND ETHICALLY

Let us assume 20% of the prospects you first touched base with have requested for more details and begin to have an in-person

the HeART of the CLOSE

conversation with you. By many industry standards 20%, is a good number.

At this second stage of the Seller's sales cycle, you work on this lead and run them through your qualifying filters of geographical location, psychological, behavioural, demographic and financial filters. You begin to invest time, money and effort on the potential buyer. Keep in mind that he will also be investing time, money and effort on you.

This is a sensitive moment that needs to be handled with outmost care. Understand that the prospect and his Triune Brain–the Rational, the Romantic and the Reactive– will be at its peak form during this interaction. The Rational Brain will be running rapid comparisons to competition in the marketplace. The Romantic Brain will have hopeful expectations. The Reactive Brain will be up with fangs, poised to fight or to take flight.

Build Rapport

Think back to how it was to have landed a first date with a woman of your dreams. (With this analogy, I may be crossing out the possibility that women, too, can initiate and land the first date with the man of their dreams. Call me old-fashioned if you wish.) Anyway, this is a crucial moment and perhaps the most important moment in **the HeART of The CLOSE** sales cycle. At this stage you talk less than the client. This is the time to give him full attention. Let him talk freely. Get to know him, learn about him, his expectations, his experiences and his real needs. In the over-a-hundred times I have run sales role-play exercises in my workshops, 90% of the play-acting salespeople always end up talking, explaining and trying to close instead of listening, probing and learning about the customer.

Returning to my analogy, less than 10% of people in the world have ever won over a spouse on their first date. It rarely happens. I remember a friend of mine sharing a story about how she went out on a date with this guy and he began to talk. For the first two hours of their evening out, he spoke about his past, his successes, his hobbies and his dreams. And then he turned to his date and said, "Hey, I have been talking all about me all night. Why don't you, now take a turn and talk about what you think of me?"

Go ahead and laugh, but be aware that it happens all the time, in life and in sales calls. Salespeople talk more about themselves when they should be discovering important insights about the prospective client.

This is a time to learn about the customer, to gently build rapport and to gain their trust. It is only when prospects recognize you are there for them (not for yourself) that they begin to give you their trust and share their stories, true needs and expectations. This is a good time to go back to chapter 3 and give the Five Fundamentals of Successful Interactions another look. This is the time to gently, carefully and deftly use the 5R questioning toolbox as explained under the 4th fundamental.

Explore and Discover Needs

In his book, What the Customer Wants You to Know, Professor Ram Charan shares the story of Unifi Inc., a textile maker in Greensboro, North Carolina. This is a company that rolled in serious trouble in the past caused by low-priced goods from China and India flooding the US markets. Professor Ram Charan writes about how the CEO of Unifi Inc. placed their Chief Information Officer in charge of sales.

the HeART of the CLOSE

Instead of utilizing traditional methods to motivate and move sales, the CIO assembled his whole sales team and asked them not sell but to instead just focus on gathering maximum information about their customers. His sales team studied the business models of each of their former customers and their prospects to learn about their supply chain as well as the businesses of their customer's customer. Day after day, the CIO pushed the sales team not sell but to learn, so they hit the road to learn everything, including the end users' consumption habits of the textile they made. Unify Inc. represented, by their sales representatives, figured out how mothers, fathers and children perceived the fabrics and the goods made from fabrics they manufactured.

Professor Ram Charan claims the process was unusual and extremely frustrating for the seasoned business-to-business salespeople. They found it unproductive and tiresome. But after several weeks of information gathering and insight accumulation about the consumers and the end customers, business began to gradually pick up. The customers, dealers and other converters of their raw material were amazed by the unusual approach of the Unifi Inc. sales team and they eagerly offered insights and tips for changing the game. The learning held relevance across industries, business models and economies engaged in all kinds of textile and fabric. Information and insights into the customer's business made up the art of giving value for the customer. Eventually, business picked up for Unify Inc. and they successfully got out of the red.

Another interesting analogy is that of a good doctor. All good doctors quickly gain their patient's trust and confidence not by popping open their medical bag and offering a cure at first sight of the patient, Doctors who take time to patiently listen, observe, and diligently analyze a patient's concerns and symptoms end up giving the most suitable prescription. They do not just offer the best prescriptions but also attend to their patient in a manner that brings about a soothing and healing.

Three Actions to Effectively Discover the Buyer's Needs

Listing down and observing these goals create value at this engagement stage of the sales process.

- **Understand the Customer's Business.**

Find out what they do and how they do it. Find out how their business systems work–where and how their products and services reach their users. Discover the kind of corporate culture they have. How are decisions made? What type of internal communication is used? How is the company doing in terms of profitability and growth? How are they perceived by their customers?

Conduct this probing carefully and diligently. The more focus and time you give to this aspect, the easier it will be to pin-point your customers' needs. Employ a combination of Research and Reflective questioning. Refrain from going, "I know exactly what you need." Even if you reach this conclusion about what exactly your customer needs, wait until your customer is willing to see the solution you visualize in your mind's eye.

- **Clarify their personal or business need.**

Remember the rule, "Never create a need where none exists."

the HeART of the CLOSE

That being said, you do need to spend time to get clarity about the customer's real needs.

Conduct the probing and interaction in such a way so the customer begins to clearly see his existing challenges. The clearer the view and insights about his needs, the easier it will be to prescribe the best medicine. Focus a lot more on using reflective questions rather than research questions at this stage. Your goal is to tap into the unseen and the unfelt or the customer's possible blind side about their need gaps.

Often times, the customers themselves try to blur the need because they don't want to expose their needy, vulnerable side or show their concern about the change and investment they'll need to make to resolve their needs. They could be exercising caution against revealing too much while you are searching deeply for details. Understand this dance and stay focused only on solving and serving rather than on selling at this stage.

- **Assess capacity and possibility of your prescribed solution.**

In the old-school, consumer goods selling profession, this goal was also referred to as a trial close. You, the modern-day conscientious, solution-finding and value-creating salesperson, want what a good doctor wants to know at this stage. A good doctor will want to assess if the treatment he is planning to prescribe will work for the patient. Will it meet her budget needs? Will it possibly stir-up side effects and allergies? Will it bring healing effectively and as quickly as needed? Does she have the strength, patience and discipline to heal with therapy or is surgical intervention the better option? A good doctor will want to know such information before prescribing treatment.

At this diagnostic stage, you can employ a combination of reflective questioning and resource assessment questioning. You may also throw in a bunch of refocused questioning towards possible healing and a solution.

Five Toolsets for Discovering Buyer Needs

- **The Five I's of Listening from Chapter 3.**

Listen deeply, actively, and with the willingness to change your assumptions and analysis.

- **Managing Perceptual Positions from Chapter 3**

Constantly find quiet ground as described and you will influence your customer to be unhurried and calm at this stage.

- **The 5-R Questioning Toolbox from Chapter 3.**

No other toolset is as powerful and effective in sales and in leading others as the power of being interested, curious, and in a learning mode about your customer.

The type of questions you ask will be reflective of your own biases in your own mindset. The quality of questions will greatly influence the accuracy of the diagnosis, and eventually, the suitability of your solution.

- **Mirror, Match and Pace**

Now this one is a sensitive, little toolset. It is a fine, delicate, handle-with-extra-care kind of technique.

Ask yourself this question. "Is it easy to build rapport with someone like you or someone quite different from you?" With this, I am not just talking about our looks and ethnicities. I am talking about how we think, how we process points, how we

the HeART of the CLOSE

express ideas and especially, how our inner energy flows.

Let's take an analogy from an experiment we've all done in our high school Physics class. Remember how one vibrating tong produced vibrations in another tong simply from putting them near each other? Now, imagine you are dancing and swaying to mellow music when another person walks up close to you and does the Rhumba. It just doesn't work. It confuses you. It turns you off.

The same happens in our business and social interactions. When we consciously harmonize our energetic vibrations and energy flow to match that of the other person, then we are apt to have good rapport.

In the traditional school of selling, this activity was referred to as finding common ground. This was usually initiated by the salesperson who, glancing around the prospects' workspace and noticing a picture of him playing golf, strikes up a conversation about golf. This worked in the USA in the 60s. In the current global world, it is a totally different story.

Today, in order to effectively mirror and match, you must generate good intentions and observe the client's energy levels. Watch, listen and feel.

When we consciously harmonize our energetic vibrations and energy flow to match that of the other person, then we are apt to have good rapport.

Is he a quick thinker, quick talker and quick mover? Does he speak in terms of examples and pictures or does he do number crunching and testimony comparisons in his head? Does he sit upright and breathe rapidly? Does he slouch and does he think slowly?

You, as a salesperson, need to be aware of his space. You need to discover the pattern to his space by observing how he sits, how he focuses, how he moves and breathes, how he inflects and modulates his voice. All these little visible, sensitive nuances will tell you how his energies dance within him. After you have a handle on the rhythm, pattern and mental footwork of his dance, then you can allow your mind, body and voice to do the same. Remember this is not mimicking but tuning in. It's known as pacing.

On the outside, at the cognitive level you are showing samples and asking questions. But on the inside, at the subjective level, you are feeling, sensing and harmonizing. His subconscious mind will sense your efforts. His Reactive Brain will smile and sashay toward you and his Romantic Brain will grant you trust and dance. While this is happening, his Reasoning Brain will be peacefully paying attention to details and offering valid and relevant detail towards a solution you are both building.

By doing what has been described in the preceding paragraphs, you will have employed the tools of mirroring and pacing. You will have built rapport and earned trust.

Now you can leave full stop. Now you can ever so gently and with absolute authenticity, leave your prospect to think along the lines of solutions and services you and your company are offering.

the HeART of the CLOSE

Here again, are my favourite words of caution, "Never create a need where none exists." Never use these tools to manipulate; use them to lead the customer to a better place at work and in his life.

- **Storytelling**

In this rapport-building and trust-earning dance, you are exploring and discovering the needs of your customers. These needs and details are not always shapes, statistics or numbers. Many times, these are fears, expectations and insights that haven't yet become crystal clear in his mind, during his analysis. When your customer discusses these fears, expectations and insights, he usually shares them with you in the form of experiences, lessons learned and stories.

Your job is to create the space for him, your customer, to open-up and start telling you as much as possible. These are 'aha!' moments of almost exploding light bulbs. These are good moments. This is where turning points take place in the sales process. This is where breakthroughs are made.

The toolset you will use is to tell stories. Share examples of your own previous experiences with customers similar to him. Tell him stories about your own buying and selling encounters or about leading at work or in life. Your objective in telling stories is to gently encourage him to narrate his stories and thus, capture the finer details of his needs and hopes. When you then eventually recommend a solution, the solution will be a perfect and a happy fit.

These five toolsets are powerful. Study them well. Use them often. You might be a little clumsy in the beginning but when you get a good grip on them, trust me, they will become

extensions of your own personality and communication style. In the next section, we will learn how to offer options toward co-creating a solution for your customers.

Stage THREE: INFLUENCE AND COVERT CONSCIENTIOUSLY

This stage of **the HeART of the CLOSE** sales process is a turning point. You have done all of the research you can. You have worked at detailing the requirements of your customer. Your customer has briefed you on his needs and expectations and both of you have invested time, money and effort into this intervention. Your customer has asked you to put it all in a proposal and he says to you, "We will see you next week, together with the production and finance team." It is time now to take it to the next level.

Offer Options

Unless you and your customer have pin-pointed a single, fail-proof solution to their needs, it is always prudent to present a few options. In the industries and businesses I have worked in, offering options was the norm, and that worked well for me. The number of choices offered to customers varies per industry. It is surprising, though, that many of them never offer more than solution.

Remember the fact that scenarios are always changing. Customers change their minds. Their life and business situations change. Or a wily competitor might sneak in a faster, cheaper and better answer to your customer's needs. These variable risks are reduced when you offer multiple options. These options set up mental perimeters for your customer but also give them space to manoeuvre.

Options can be offered in many ways. *The HeART of the CLOSE* will focus on two ways: options offered in a written proposal and options given in person by way of a presentation.

Formula For Written Proposals:

- **Place** yourself in the mind of the buyer. Recognize and note at which mental stage of the buying process she might be.

- **Plan** the depth and flow of the proposal before you begin writing.

- **Open up** with sincere congratulatory or complimentary remarks about their business, brand and plans for innovation or expansion.

- **Gently flow** into an explanation of the needs you have discovered and analyzed from your meetings with them. Be clear, objective and open to corrections made about their needs. Summarize the needs while highlighting key results from the impact of utilizing solutions offered by you/your company.

- **Describe** the solutions and their explicit benefits, supported by details on the depth and scope of the features.

- **Offer options**; NOT just one, fail-proof, best solution. Take your one, fail-proof, best solution and then create, at least, three variances of the same solution by changing the scope, the timings and advantages in each of the three options. Offering options is an invitation for your

customer to participate in finding the solution. It creates a sense of ownership in their minds.

- **State one** single price offer for each of the three solutions together with two possible ways for them to pay. Offer incentives if the payment plans are in your favor.

- **Follow through** with the long-term, monetary and performance advantages of your proposal.

- **Never end** a proposal with a "final take it or leave it" type of tone. Keep your tone open and invitational so they don't feel cornered and uncomfortable discussing business with you.

- **Peg a validity period** to your proposal and its terms because the offer you make now may change over time, most certainly if the client takes a long while to decide.

Purpose-Driven Presentations

A slightly different set of skills is needed when personally presenting a proposal to a group of people. How to make a pitch was covered earlier in this chapter under Initiating Dialogue. The next paragraphs will talk about presentations, working the room, managing your visuals and facilitating forums

Let's say you are to present in a small room with an audience of five or seven people. Let's say you have spent days preparing your presentation well. You have prepared in a way that engages the Romantic, and the Reactive Brain but also impresses the analytical needs of the Reasoning Brain. Let's also say you have not just prepared mentally and emotionally, but have

the HeART of the CLOSE

also practiced. You have tried and tested the proposal with your manager, with your colleagues, and your family. You have worked out all the kinks and loopholes, and you are ready to go to the market with it.

The 3Ps of Powerful Impact

Here are practices you can do so your customers more easily accept your proposal. I call this the 3-P method of powerfully impacting the room.

P1 - Plant Yourself

Plant yourself in a position in the room where you have the widest view of the room. This is not at the head of the table or the CEO's chair but in another seat which is open to all, open to guests like you.

Come early to seat yourself in that position. If you are going to stand up and speak, then pre-locate the sweet spot where your view is not obstructed and where most of your customers have a good view of you. Come early to get the feel of the place, to plant yourself comfortably, and so your anxiety level and emotions simmer down. Come early and find yourself quiet ground.

When you are calm and settled in, you will have higher awareness and can better respond to your customer's queries.

P2 - Pause for a While

Starting to talk as soon as you walk in demonstrates an attitude of being focused on the content and not so much on context. Despite a fast, global business culture, this can be considered

disrespectful of those present. It shows you don't care about what their state of mind might be at that moment.

A pause allows others to also settle down and find quiet ground. If from this silence, you then start talking slowly, you will arrive at a better position to mirror, pace and lead your audience.

In that moment of silence before you start filling the room with the sound of your voice, you will, firstly, have more time to mentally review and edit what you are planning to present. Secondly, you can make eye contact and kinaesthetically acknowledge the presence of all other "human beings" in the room. It is an act of respect that also allows you to gather your thoughts one last time.

P3 - Project with Power

I agree 100% with keeping your tone conversational and your presentations interactive. I am all for it. I also want to add that all eyes are on you when you are proposing or presenting. Your objective is to convince your audience to change their minds for the better and to impress them so they move toward progress.

While keeping your tone even and your demeanour humble, you also have to amplify your presence and project your voice. Sit up, stand tall, breathe well, look people in the eye and speak to the person farthest away from you. Use extra energy and power.

Projecting your voice and managing your sales presentation puts across an air of authority and conviction. Your diagnosis of the customer's needs may be accurate and your products may be the best in the marketplace. But if you do not demonstrate authority or conviction with your voice and demeanour then you will not be able to influence or sell.

These 3 Ps combined will optimally equip you to manage and work a room, regardless of its size, shape, or location. It works for an audience of one or a thousand.

PowerPoint Do or Die, Managing Your Visuals

Technology is considered a boom to our age because it has made a lot of processes so much easier. We can connect with people across the world in real-time, via multiple modes and at negligible or zero cost. We can send documents, images, audio and video files across the oceans at the click of a mouse. The downside is this technical digital world can and does take away the richness of organic, human touch.

In my workshops, I have many times seen people get all tied-up wanting to know how to handle this boon and downside combination of technology. When to use it and when not to use it. How much to learn, how much to depend on it, and exactly how to leverage it. These are the questions on people's minds all the time.

Here are my tips on what to do when using technology for sales presentations. These are just quick tips. The subject is wide and its elements so numerous. People have written volumes about it. In addition, the number of technical applications in the area of presentations grows and multiples day by day.

Quick Tips on the Use of Presentation Applications such as PowerPoint, Keynote, Prezi:
- **Keep it simple and easy.** You don't want your client or you to be sucked into the wonders of the technology.

the HeART of the CLOSE

- **Use clear, simple images** instead of complicated details or volumes of text.
- **Display ONLY data** and objects you cannot explain verbally.
- Explanations, examples and **stories need to be narrated** orally, not visually displayed.
- **Show numbers**, graphs, charts, flow diagrams and statistics wherever needed.
- **Forget rules** such as the 5 words x 3 lines etc. The size, color and shape of all text, objects and images must simply be such that the farthest person in the room can see them without straining his eyes.
- If you can (and you feel you can) **connect, engage** and make a better impact without PowerPoint then do away with it.

The Necessary Forum

Another question I get asked frequently is how I manage interruptions and questions during my presentations. Experienced salespeople will smile and tell you that interruptions and questions can be an indication of interest in your proposal and your products. They can be great buying signals from your buyer.

Here's what I want to tell you about managing questions and forums. Welcome them. Be happy these questions are being asked. Questions do not reflect an interruption or a lack of conviction in your proposal. Think positive and look at them as your customer's desire to know more, to learn more before making a decision. The more questions are raised, the sooner the decision will appear. It shows that you are moving in the right direction into a close.

Despite full product and industry knowledge and all the research you might have done about the market and the customer's needs, it is impossible to be 100% accurate. Even the world's best doctor needs to take a second look, do another test, and try different prescriptions before he hits the nail on the head. When the customers ask questions they are working at aligning your recommendations to their business needs and challenges. It is a dance where all the footwork needs to match and complement. Thus, answer questions to the best of your ability. Respond to their Reasoning Brain's analytical needs.

Pointers for Managing the Forum:

- Share facts with the Reasoning Brain, give hope to the Romantic Brain and alleviate doubts in the Reactive Brain. If you have visual aids and samples, use these freely to demonstrate.

- When a question is raised by an individual, answer him and draw others into the picture also. If you have a technical team member on your side, let him support your answers.

- If you don't have the answer and need to verify it, admit it. "I do not have the answer and will need to get back to you."

- Never laugh off a question. Never lie. And totally avoid putting down your competition. It reflects upon your character.

- Be honest, be authentic and straightforward and focus on fully educating your prospect and creating value.

the HeART of the CLOSE

At this Influence with Conscientiousness stage in **the HeART of the CLOSE** sales process, the forum will bring you 70% - 80% nearer to the final close and towards a win-win outcome.

Prescribe Solutions And Manage Objections

Questions can be challenging and demanding at this stage of influencing with conscientiousness. In the old-school of selling these were referred to as "objections." I am not partial to negativity of thought or any single word that carries negativity in its core or in its etymology. The school of thought and the discipline I come from believes positivity, appreciation and affirmation exist in the subtlety of the words.

Let's say customers need a little more clarity, perspective and convincing about your solutions. Let's say customers have expectations and some of them may be unrealistic and borne out of simplistic reasons. Our job as ethical, value-creating salespeople is to manage these expectations, or what others may call objections. Aside from the technical aspects of features and benefits most so-called objections are about time and money. Many times these objections are from lack of clarity, unfounded fears and skewed perspectives.

Three approaches in handling objections, managing expectations and exploring solutions.

a. Pre-frame the Expectations.

Let's say as your company's sales representative, you know the industry, the brand, the product, and the market niche you cater to. You know the unique benefits your product and services

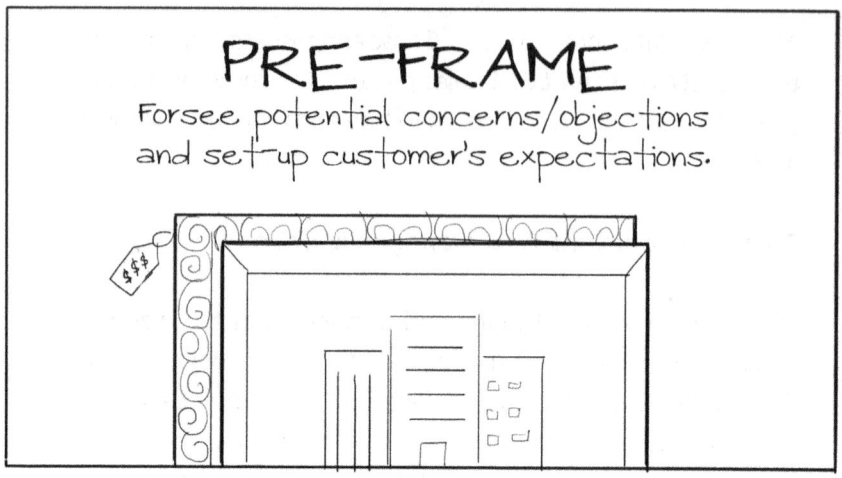

or what makes it better than other similar products in the marketplace. You also know your price may be a few notches above the rest due to the positive features of your product, service and brand. Many of the prospects who worked with you until this stage of the sales process may still be concerned about cost. That is perfectly normal. Different people have different mindsets about how they use money. Your job is to manage this possibility.

You can Pre-frame the possible objection. A Pre-frame is a scenario frame you present before p mentioning the tag price so that the tag price is perceived in relation to that scenario frame. It's like letting your customer handle a hand-carved, satin laden jewellery box before you drop a diamond stud into it.

The way it can be done, for example, in selling high-end condominiums, is by saying, "Glad you have formed up your mind to invest in this upscale neighbourhood, yes?" This is bound to bring forth a "Yes" answer as well as relieve any tension or fear from your prospect's mind.

the HeART of the CLOSE

You say this instead of saying, "By the way we are highly priced, you know?" That would instil fear and caution about what's coming up. It also is tantamount to shot selling or being out of synch with your product and product value.

The example is specific to the residential property industry, but many creative ideas can be taught through and tested before applying them in other kinds of businesses/industry. Use language and its impact deftly while keeping in mind the principles of congruence and ecology.

b. Reframe Objections.

Objections are usually about perceptions of time and money. A little adjustment on how potential buyers view things can get us closer to getting the sale. Say a prospect mentions that the condominium you are selling is at least 20% higher in price than another one 20 kilometres away from the city.

Instead of being floored by this fact, a salesperson could say, "Would the 20% still appear higher if say, for the next five

REFRAME
Keep the content
and change the context.

years you spend 45 minutes in traffic each way every day?" Or, "Would that 20% still look higher if you'd consider the thousands of dollars you'd save every month?"

There's a good chance you will have created a different chain of thought in the buyer's mind after they've raised such an objection.

c. De-frame Objections.

This one is different and needs to be handled with care. Like a re-frame it is also employed after an objection is raised. It is tantamount to smashing a picture frame that doesn't do justice to the picture or in this case, the paradigm held in it.

So an example of this might be, say your condominium buying prospect says, "I'm afraid I may not be able to convince my mother about the payment terms."

Your response can be an open-ended question, "What are we

DE-FRAME

Challenge misconceived perceptions.
Remove the frames/fears totally.

the HeART of the CLOSE

talking about here, the terms or the fact that you might not be able to convince your mother?" Again, this will get you right back on track and back into the sales process.

Let me say this one more time. As a salesperson you are doing the ethical dance. If you suspect that your client's fears are real, then you, as an ethical salesperson, need to take the righteous path and refrain from trying to push ahead with that sale.

The examples I have cited are hypothetical and extreme. You are the expert in your industry. Practice and play around with de-framing objectives relevant to your business.

At this point, the third stage of the buying process comes to an end. You have connected, you have engaged and you have handed your prospect a perfect proposal. You have filled in all the data needs of the Reasoning Brain, have created expectations and desire for the Romantic Brain and allayed the concerns of the Reactive Brain.

It is time to step back and ease away from the activity. It is time to pause, contemplate and practice patiently waiting until the buyer and his three brains begin to hum the same tune. It is time to step back and let the buying come into its own for your business prospect. Ease back just a bit, just as a master painter steps away and gives his work a critical, contemplative, big-picture look before picking up the brush and the palette one more time. At this point in **the HeART of the CLOSE** dance of selling, you are more than 80% closer to making a win-win deal. Before an ultimate close, comes a bit of negotiation, a bit of formalizing the sales, followed by delivery and service.

Stage FOUR: ACQUIRE AUTHENTIC COMMITMENT

So here we are within visible distance of the ultimate close. This is an exciting stage. It is quite close to the next level but it is not yet the close. If we have, so far, performed all the steps well, played our cards right and put passion and purpose into this process, then acquiring authentic commitment should be

Yet, even when our product, pricing and proposal are perfect, our customer wants to fine tune the purchase and the partnership. This is normal and part of a buyer's due diligence. Sometimes, it is just human nature to negotiate further. It is quite similar to having impressed, romanced and proposed to the love of your life with a diamond studded ring and she says "Yes!" But after she says yes, she still wants to discuss prenuptials and the marriage plans. That is appropriate and serves both parties well. Yes, finding and keeping Miss Right has many parallels with doing good business.

Negotiating Nuances

Here are some guides to negotiation to help you toward the final deal:

a.   Know Exactly What You Want and can Give.

This is the negotiation-skills' version of "Know thyself." Going in casually and unprepared while hoping to step out of this stage by chance is tantamount to taking a walk into Mike Tyson's ring and coming out carrying the champion's belt wrapped in a bunch of daisies.

Make a clear list of things you would like to gain. Don't hesitate

the HeART of the CLOSE

to come out a winner. Win-win is always a good thing, but a big-time win-win is much better. Similarly, make a clear list of what you can give in terms of money, time, quality, quantities and warranties. That means how long and how far you will stay responsible and supportive of your product. Lifetime warranties are ideal but realistic costs of product design and delivery need to be carefully factored in.

Run this list through with your manager and colleagues. If needed, rehearse a negotiation. Like Shakespeare wrote, "all the world is a stage," and all successful negotiations are just that…brilliant performances.

b. Talk about Money Last.

Refrain from talking numbers at the initial stage of the selling process. Usually, the knee-jerk strategy of the buyer is to go for the question, "How much?" or "What's your best price?"

Consider that your proposal is of loosely-held-together parts and you are trying to fit this into your buyer's need while pushing all the other parts in. You will need to first get a stake and then anchor in for the climb. Hold off on all money discussions until everything else is a yes. This is risky, but risky is where increased profitability and growth lies. Avoid words like "it is negotiable", or "we can talk about the price"' or "we do offer discounts," etc. This belittles your product, your proposal, and the total value proposition to the buyer.

c. Move from Strength to Strength.

After you have held back from talking about money for a while and buyer responses are positive, you can enhance goodwill by giving them a few extras if possible. Next, look through the buyers profile and seek what might be of a minor cost to him but quite valuable to you, and then ask for it. This is win-win in practice. This is moving from strength to strength.

I sell training programs where often, the client seeks a different subject matter or uncommon training schedules but doesn't have the budget to pay more. In this case, instead of talking about money, I offer something of equal value. I ask for an advertisement that more or less matches the value I am providing. Thus, the second negotiation tip–move from strength to strength–means if you give them something, then ask for something as well. When they give you something, go ahead and give them something back in return. Just see to it that the give and take is balanced and not tipping heavily in either party's favor.

Make sure too that your client never makes any deal under duress or pressure. If you take advantage of a moment of weakness in your client, you are being unfair. Likewise, if you compromise on any transaction and give in to the client's demands without really wanting to, you are not moving from strength to strength. Like my good ol' teacher D.N. Irani used to say, "Fair exchange, never a robbery."

d.   Sustain Your Stamina for the Long Haul.

Value creation is a dance between the buyer and you, and this dance can take long. Statistics show that 80% of the gains in negotiation occur in the final 20% of the time people spend at the negotiating table. So, hold up your energies as far as you can as the best will come at the end. Practice patience and resilience in conversations. Rushing through this Acquiring Authentic

the HeART of the CLOSE

5 Never count your money at the table.

Sustain stamina. 80% of trasanctions comes about in the last 20% of the negotiation cycle

4

Move from strength to strength. Don't decide under duress and let client choose well.

3

Refrain from responding to "how much?" until the need-solution fit looks increasingly promising and client gets eager to buy.

2

Know exactly what you want to get and what you can give in the transaction

1

Commitment stage can be harmful as you may overlook some finer details and come out the loser in the bargain. If your buyer is hurrying you, then chances are they have an edge over you. At this time, step back and look at the bigger view to find that edge. If needed, take a finite walk to the washroom and back. Pausing, breathing, and taking time off can be a tactic.

I was once sitting across an events producer in Vietnam. He had the marketing and event managing machinery for Asia and I had the content and the talent. During the negotiations across the dinner table, our horns locked over my daily professional fee. He was a few hundred dollars away from my ideal price. I needed business and I suspected he needed it too. When our horns locked, I asked to go to the washroom. There, I paused to think through every systemic aspect and the positive ripple effects of the potential partnership.

When I returned and sat down at the table, I realized he too had paused to put his three brains to work, and he agreed to give me a slight raise. That pause allowed me to get what I wanted without actually having to ask for it. Keeping my excitement under a polite smile, I thanked him.

e.   Never Count Your Money while at the Table

Whenever possible and if your industry practices allow it, do not show the cost breakdown of your proposal. Doing this turns your value proposition into salami. The buyer may separate what works for him and leave you with little to nothing. Amazon doesn't tell you where they make their money. They sell you books at less than a dollar, but their income is in the packaging and the postage.

the HeART of the CLOSE

Likewise, heed Kenny Rogers warning about "never counting your money while sitting at the table". When my client in Vietnam gave me what I wanted, I didn't jump up and down and tell him how thrilled I was. That would have created remorse on his side and our partnership would have been impaired.

whenever possible and if your industry practices allow it, do not show the cost breakdown of your proposal.

So, keep up a poker face, trust in your product, trust in the value proposition, and then always deliver more than you commit.

Formalize Sales and Document Before Delivery.

Paperwork is important, especially so in project-based or large business-to-business sales. You and your buyer have both invested quite a bit into this transaction and it is time to put it in black and white. During documentation, get all the terms and agreements right. Have both parties verify and clarify the fine print, before you place your thumbprints or hit the "submit button".

Remember this and note it well, "The value of a product or service depreciates the moment delivery is done." Even if the product is a diamond, the moment you deliver it to your customer, you already sink-in handling, packaging and delivery costs. The moment a car is driven out of the showroom, it already becomes a used car. Thus the cost of all products and services must be figured in and collected as early as possible, if not before delivery.

You have now closed the deal, but **the HeART of the CLOSE** isn't over. You need to go to the next level. You have to serve wholeheartedly to build and sustain the relationship.

Stage FIVE: SERVE WHOLEHEARTEDLY

Early in the 80's, my partner, Robert Uy from Paramount Apparels, Inc., and I had closed a deal with Sandra Greenberg of Cottonwood Fines of New York for five thousand dozens of embroidered tops to be shipped the following summer to the USA.

When the goods were in production, Sandra Greenberg with her quality control inspectors flew in to the Philippines to perform a cursory inspection. While inspecting, the Cottonwood team found several flaws in the product like skipped stitches, wrinkled hems, oil stains, etc.,

Sandra raised the issues, which Robert thought were minor issues she should let pass. This quick conversation I was privy to and the lop-sided views held by both parties have stayed on my mind. In defense of his company's production, Robert said, "Your quality is too high!" Sandra straightened up, looked around at all the people standing and declared, "As far as I'm concerned and as far as I know, there is only one kind of quality and that is the quality we agreed upon." Robert had no reply to such a statement, although I suspected he really didn't agree with Sandra's opinion.

I look back today to that exchange and the perspectives held by the two parties. Sandra came from a high content, task-oriented work culture and Robert came from a high context, relationship-oriented work culture. The former believed the finest details of

the HeART of the CLOSE

any contract must be followed to the letter. The latter thought one must gratefully accept what becomes available. Beyond the two perspectives, it was to me a resounding lesson in keeping one's commitments to agreements made and delivering solutions that fit your customer's needs.

This is one aspect of service beyond sales in the 5th stage of the sales cycle. If you, the seller, do not meet all the commitments, then you shall not have served your customer fully or whole-heartedly.

Nurture Their Every Whim

Macy's, the biggest department store in the heart of New York, is a place to go to when you want to shop in New York. It occupies more than 200, 000 square meters and has been gracing that corner of the city for more than 110 years. It carries the best of consumer brands from across the world and it's considered a landmark of success and service in the US. Macy's service policy is an old one and they take pride on the impact it has on its brand and reputation.

Let's say you buy one of their US$ 1,000 Italian-made suits, take it home and then wear it the next day. At breakfast your seven-year-old darling daughter says, "Daddy, that suit is so dark." And you go "You don't like the color, honey?" She replies, "No, daddy. It makes you look angry." From that conversation, you change into another suit for work, and a few days later you bring the suit back to Macy's. The sales-attendant in Macy's will go, "Oh, sir, that's alright if you have brought it back. Did it not fit well?" You honestly reply, "Oh, no, no. that's not it. It's just that my 7-year-old daughter doesn't like it." The attendant looks up at you and smiles with a twinkle in his eye and says, "Surely sir, I bet she knows what she is talking about. Would you like to find another color?" You reply, "Oh, no. I am in a bit of a rush. May I just get a refund?" And after just a bit of paperwork you will surely step out of Macy's with cash in your pocket or the credit back into your card. The whole incident is soon out of your mind as you head back home to your family.

Macy's has been doing this for decades and most of you, if not the whole world, know about Macy's service quality and commitment to serve its customers. In the fast, closely connected world of today, Macy's is not the only business known for such service quality. Thousands of businesses across the world stand solidly behind their products and services. They provide a lifetime warranty that supports their promise of forever.

Nourish the Relationship

The second aspect of serving wholeheartedly dictates that you, the business and service provider, must continuously stand behind your product through full utilization and optimal enjoyment of your client.

I was once with a bunch of colleagues flying back to Manila from Cebu in the Philippines and while at the airport, we walked into to a place called The Toast Box. I ordered tuna sandwich and lemonade. Upon ordering, I wondered aloud if my sandwich came with a few potato chips on the side. The waitress, Janice, replied that it did not come with chips but added she'd be happy to go buy some for me from another establishment nearby. I was a bit perplexed about their policy and wondered how she could leave without the manager's approval. Nevertheless, I said,

"Well, that would be nice of you. Can you get me a small bag of Lay's Salt and Vinegar flavoured chips?" but before I could give her the money for the chips, she was gone. She was actually gone for quite a while, considering that Mactan Airport in Cebu, Philippines is not so big.

When she eventually came back, I thanked her and inquired gently about what took her so long. She said she had to step out the airport for the chips. I was amazed. I knew there was the issue of not seeking permission and even some risk from not following policy in the adventure she took. But I did appreciate dedicated service.

Not all businesses lean back as much to serve customers but we must stretch as far as possible, as often as possible, in the service of our clients. Only then can we truly go the extra mile and constantly set new standards of sales and service excellence.

Thus, the three takeaways of this story of exceptional service are:
- Serve with the commitment to quality. Never cut corners or expect your customers to compromise.
- Deliver the proverbial extra mile whenever and wherever possible to set new standards of performance.
- Stand behind your products and services consistently as far as you can to become the legend that Macy's is in New York

Following these principles allows us to continuously surpass standards of sales and service excellence and create new benchmarks for building and nourishing relationships with our customers. We will constantly and consistently fill the needs of a changing world and raise the standards of life.

CLOSE AN ICE-CREAM CONE

As I wrap up this section on the sales cycle and the five-stage process of connecting, engaging, influencing, acquiring, and serving our customers through **the HeART of the CLOSE**, I'd like to talk about a story that kept popping up in my mind throughout the writing of this chapter. The story featured in one of the issues of Reader's Digest in the late 60's which I read as a kid in India. The article was called "How to Eat an Ice-Cream Cone."

I looked up and found the article written by Lawrence Rust Hills, author of "How to Do Things Right" by Bantam Books. The article was initially published in the August 1968 issue of New Yorker before being published in Reader's Digest.

When you first get an ice cream cone, L. Rust Hills advises you hold it gently somewhere in the middle with your thumb and three fingers and your pinky finger sticking out. Step away and stand apart from the usual crowd that surrounds the ice cream vendor.

Size up the ice cream; do a quick scan of its weight, center of gravity, tilt and its melting state all in relation to the environment around you. Bend forward by 25 degrees and raise your elbow of the hand that holds the ice cream so your full arm is nearly parallel to the ground.

Survey the sides of the cone for dripping goblets and compare it to the bottom tip where there usually is a hole. The danger of an ice-cream crash landing is possible at either of these ends so do a quick mental assessment and choose which side to save first (top or bottom).

Hold the little cone up in air as you would hold up a glass of champagne for a toast. Then, let that cone drop down into your throat. Gulp! You have a close.

With the decision made, remain bent forward by a maximum of 25 degrees and then stick out your tongue, rapidly licking for damage control. Move rapidly from one end to another until the threat of falling is reduced, then straighten up and take a quick breath.

Again, bend forward by 25 degrees and work on the dollops of cream on top, licking it in laps as you swirl the cone around between the thumb and the fingers, pinky finger still sticking out. Round and round goes the ice-cream cone, as you occasionally check the bottom tip. In about two minutes, you will have balanced all the sides of the cream. The danger will have diminished, but is not totally gone.

Next, start taking kiss like bites of the cream and give the top a gentle push with your lips. This will push the ice cream deeper into the cone where it is many times safer. You can now take a moment to look around if there's competition beating you to winning the ice cream eating challenge or if someone may snatch your business away.

You are now nearing a close. Gently continue nibbling and licking until the ice cream shrinks down to a size a bit bigger than your thumb. The deal is almost done. Because you were focused on the gentle handling of the ice-cream, you haven't

realized you are now standing up straight, having relinquished your bent-down position some time ago.

The penultimate stage of this hearty ice-cream eating process is to hold the little cone up in air as you would hold up a glass of champagne for a toast. Then, let that cone drop down into your throat. Gulp! You have a close. You've done it! The ice-cream cone is happy and so are you, not just for the moment but for a long time after and until it is time for another ice cream cone in this delicious journey called, **the HeART of the CLOSE**.

CHAPTER 5

MANAGING THE SALES FUNCTION

If you have happily read until this page then it implies that you like the business of selling and hopefully too, that you like this book. Selling gives you a high. You like the freedom, you like making money with your efforts and you like working with people. You also probably like eating ice cream out of a cone without letting a drop hit the ground.

ONE: PEOPLE MANAGEMENT AND THE SALES AND MARKETING SALSA

Congratulations! From being a sales-executive, you are now managing a team of sales executives. Good! You have reason to celebrate. But here's a bit of a reminder to keep your feet on the ground, "With added powers, come added responsibility." On the dance floor of selling, you are not just concerned with "mirroring, pacing and leading" your clients. You also have to deal with top management and others in finance, operations and human resources.

From just working with customers and clients, your perceptions will now have to take a broader perspective. You will have to sharpen your entrepreneurial skills and convert your unit into a profit center. You will have to hone your creative

thinking, risk taking, decision making and allocation of scarce resources. Your top management will expect and push you to see the big picture, to think strategically, and to deliver systemic results over the long term.

The systems, strategies and techniques in the next paragraphs will equip you to perform effectively and ethically as a sales manager. Let's just take a few of these entities and recognize what needs to be done.

Sales and Marketing

Far too many big and small enterprises, globally, lack the ability to clearly distinguish the roles and responsibilities of the Sales and the Marketing departments.

Decades ago, there were efforts to set clear distinctions in their functions. Today, just as it is a fine line that separates sales and service, the line between sales and marketing departments has also become blurred. Nevertheless, some functional highlights and required competencies are illustrated on the Table below.

The job of the marketer in simple terms involves taking a helicopter view of the company and the product and then deciding where to direct and position them. The concept of

the HeART of the CLOSE

- Managing Time and Resources
- Setting Goals and Training
- Partnering with Other Departments
- Keeping Track of Progress, Building Teams
- Aligning, Planning, and Forecasting
- Managing Territories
- Coaching Salespersons

COMPETENCY REQUIRED		
MARKETING		SALES
Positioning	KNOWLEDGE	Knowhow & Process
Strategic	THINKING STYLE	Tactical & Agile
Brand building	PEOPLE SKILLS	Value Creating

brand representing product and the product living up to its brand-name is dynamism in action, a living thing. It has to find its place in a crowded world and it has to have a character and an identity in the consumer's mind. That is the job of the marketing department. It looks at how the company is doing and more importantly, at how it is perceived by consumers and competitors.

From the high perch on the helicopter, marketers also perform the job of the look-out scout. They gather data, monitor opinions and trends and stir up a buzz about the enterprise and its products. If from the helicopter they find fertile ground, they write-up good seeds in the form of blogs, articles, chats, forums, press releases and scatter them from the sky.

You, in the sales department, are on the ground. You have face-to-face contact with the customers. Thus, all your encounters are up close and conversational. You have to live with and understand the fact that you cannot succeed without the support of the helicopter view provided by the marketing department. It's a dance and both of you have to hold each other tight. If they don't locate fertile ground and don't scatter seeds, then you cannot pluck the fruits of success.

the HeART of the CLOSE

But while it is a dance of equals, it is harder to measure and analyze the marketing department's contributions compared to the efforts you and your sales team make.

Here are a few practices to collaborate fully and generate better results for your team and the whole enterprise.

- Dialogue, as often and as deeply as possible, with the marketing department. Learn about trends, what the competition is doing and the type of consumer insights your products and services create in the marketplace.

- Utilize the tools, collaterals, social media access created and maintained by the marketing department and pass them feedback from the feed so they can adjust and improve their campaigns.

- Provide actual sales statistical composition and reports. This is valuable fodder for the marketing department, especially when the sales department is descriptive and diligent in transferring this information, which then benefits all.

Sales and Other Departments

I know from experience that all the efforts made by the sales department will go to waste if these are not supported by the production, operations, logistics, and finance or service departments. This painful fact is true, both for business-to-consumer goods and for business-to-business capital goods and projects.

It is because of challenges in the areas of production, delivery, and accounting services that many good sales people abandon ship. They are the face of the business they represent, after all, and a loss of face with the clients is nearly impossible to gain back.

Two suggestions for eliminating or lessening the challenges from other departments:

- Partner up and cooperate with production, project-delivery and service to get their realistic commitments which your team members can confidently offer to your customers.

- Talk firmly to convince top management when bringing up issues for discussion. The sales department is the driver of the train of enterprise. It carries all other departments. No sales means no cash flow and no cash flow can put an enterprise to death. Bring this to the awareness of the top management and shareholders because they own the train that you drive.

Your Sales Team and You

As a successful salesperson you and your own performance was top priority. As a sales manager, your sales team is now your prime responsibility. You will need to create an atmosphere where success can be bred and nurtured. Most of your work will be done with your team. You will have to equip yourself with new disciplines and people skills.

I call it people management savvy. But you can also think of it as a car production assembly line, where various parts are assembled by different technicians. A car that will take days to assemble if done by an individual can be assembled in a matter

the HeART of the CLOSE

of hours by a team. Your job is to bring out as many cars as possible in a better, faster and less costly way.

Train Them in **the HeART of the CLOSE** Process

Let them have a fine understanding of the five stages of the sales process; connect, engage, influence, acquire and serve. Highlight the meaningful analogy of "how to eat an ice-cream cone," a few licks and a few bites at a time until the proverbial close becomes an inevitable occurrence. Do away with the caricature of the sales manager screaming, "I need more sales! I need more closes! I need more businesses!" What you need is a disciplined, motivated sales team who is informed about what to do and say at the right time using the minimum amount of time and resources.

Educate Them with Product, Business and Market Knowledge

It is tempting to say here that you and your team must first find and hire the right talent. Instead, let's go with the assumption that just like you did not get to choose your family members, you also did not get to choose your team members.

Orient them in the detail on the features, benefits and advantages of your company's products. Also do not hesitate to expose them to the services and strategies of the competition. Salespeople want honesty and thoroughness. They also expect their manager to trust them.

Make them aware of the marketplace trends, the culture and the types of buyers. Educate them in the macro perspective of country economics and outlook. You don't want your sales person plugging away high-end luxury goods in an economy where people are struggling to buy basic needs.

Teach Them to Set SmartER Goals

It is well understood that S.M.A.R.T. stands for Specific, Measurable, Attainable, Relevant, and Time-bound goals. Now **the HeART of the CLOSE** will add E and R to make it SMARTer.

What do we mean when we say specific, measurable, and time-bound? Let's look at the illustration as we speak.

Let's talk about specificity and review the power of intention as discussed in chapter 2. Answer the question: What do you want? Take the necessary pause, think deeply, and answer the question. What is it you truly want?

Answering "I don't want to be living on a month-to-month income" does not help. Your three brains will have an internal conversation and will bring up an image of, "living on a month-to-month income." The triune brain will not know how to negate an idea or image. It does not know the concept of "Don't" want. For example, if I tell you not to think of a pink elephant, what does your triune brain do? It brings up a picture of a pink elephant in your mind. It can try but will be unsuccessful in erasing it.

So, when stating a goal, state it in a positive statement. Instead of the above negative statement, recast the thought to something like I want enough personal cash reserves to sustain my living style for at least 5 months. Now that is positively stated, but it is ambiguous. You need to give it specificity. You get the picture? Question: What is it you really want? Wrong answer: "I don't

the HeART of the CLOSE

want to be living on a month-to-month basis." Right answer: "I want to have enough to live by for 5 months. Right, specific answer: "I want a consistent, available cash of $20,000 in my bank." Specify the answer by stating $20, 000. That is a specific want expressed as a goal. It can get more detailed by expressing the name of the bank but we can settle for this much specificity for now.

Now, let's talk about the measurability of a set goal. With measurability, we need to answer the question of "How?" Question: How do you get that $20, 000 as a consistent cash reserve? Answer: We get there by saving up $4,000 every month or $1,000 every week. The goal setter has answered the specific and measurable part of the goal setting process.

The next detail we need to fill in is the question of being attainable. Question: Can you save up $4000 per month? Answer: Yes. Question: How exactly? Answer: I will dine out twice a month instead of twice a week. I will take the bus to work every day instead of a cab. I will limit personal shopping expenses from 2,000 a month to 1,000 a month. I will move into an apartment costing 1, 500 a month instead of the one I am currently renting at 2, 500 a month. I will connect with 20 new prospects every week. This is how you probe and detail answers to the question "Is the goal attainable? It can be further drilled down to finer details.

The Relevancy portion of the goal setting taps into the Romantic and the Reactive brain parts of the triune brain and it answers the question "Why?" in the goal setting process. Question: Why is the goal important to you? Wrong answer #1: Well, as I said, I don't want to be living on a month-to-month cash flow. Wrong answer #2: I want to be more successful than the Joneses. Right

answer: I believe the security of having the available cash flow will keep me peaceful, happy and more productive.

The Relevancy part of the goal setting process must have meaning and value to the goal setter and must be an intention and desire initiated by her. You, as a sales manager, can set business targets and quarterly sales quotas for your salesperson, but the desire needs to be ignited by her. You can assess the potential and coach her into clarity of thought and creativity of planning, but she needs to take all the actions – internal and external.

The question of a goal being time-bound is partially answered when we test the size and the attainability of the goal.

So your salesperson needs to put aside an exact amount of $20,000 in 5 months. This is her personal goal. Part of the work that needs to be done to attain this goal falls under your supervision. That is the part about her making connections with 20 new prospects every week. This is important to you as far as your team's performance is concerned, but it is still not S.M.A.R.T. from your perspective because her connecting with 20 new prospects on its own will not hit your company's sales targets. We will cover that later in forecasting, planning, and managing the whole sales function.

Now, let's move on to the "ER" part in SMARTer goal setting. "ER" stands for "Ecologically Right" goals. Let's look back at the two principles of congruence and ecology as discussed in Chapter 4.

By the SMART process of goal setting, we've covered the internal values and the external actions the goal setting salesperson needs to take towards congruency. The Ecologically Right parameter of goal setting means as the individual passionately and persistently chases after and achieves her goal, it should not cause stress, suffering or damage to herself, to any other relationships, and to systemic linkages.

For example, while chasing the goal of saving up $20,000 in 5 months, she takes up commuting by bus rather than driving to work and this is physically challenging and exhausting for her. At the end of the 5 months, she does save up $20,000 but gets ill and needs medical care and hospitalization. This also uses up $7000 off her savings. Her goal was achieved but harm has been done. The goals were SMART but not SMARTer.

Likewise, the sales manager has to look out for the many systemic effects of motivating his team to drive up performance and improve profitability.

Neuro Persuasions

As a manager of sales, it is ideal and will do you good in the eyes of your team when your level of competence and knowledge is at a higher, sharper edge than theirs.

Obviously, you might have had more years of work experience and/or education. This additional information on how markets and customers think will give you that respected edge as well as offer you insights into social neuropsychology to sell even better.

Group minds or let's say group brains have a structure quite similar to that of an individual triune brain. Yes, they are similar but not exactly the same. Group brains also have a three-tiered structure of the Reasoning, Romantic, and the Reactive

brain. You can catch these brains in action when you look at an audience watching a movie of high drama and high action like the Titanic. You can see the audience taking in the glitz and glamour with a rational mind and you will notice their eyes moistening and their lips smiling when love and hope takes form on the silver screen. You can actually see all eyes widen, in unison in fear when people die and the great ship sinks into the ocean. Large groups are also driven by good reasoning, romance, and deep abject fear coming from the group's Reactive brain.

Let's revisit a big marketing campaign in 1985. Remember "the New Coke" marketing promotion of 1985 when after nearly a hundred years of selling the classic drink, Coke ran a survey for a newer, sweeter drink? The survey results as tapped from the Reasoning and the Romantic group brain came forth with the conclusion that the Coke-drinking world would love the newer, sweeter drink. The survey results were so good, in fact, that they claimed the new Coke would crush the hold of Pepsi on the marketplace and just wipe it out completely.

When the new Coke eventually launched, it turned out to be one of the worst marketing disasters of all time. Consumers, organizations and states rejected and condemned the new drink. They couldn't do away with their sentimental attachment to the "old drink". The Reactive organizational brain felt threatened and cheated—no amount of Reasoning and Romancing could convince customers on the new Coke.

Coke had to finally call off the "new Coke" campaign. They pulled out and trashed all the existing stocks of the new Coke. They went back to the classic Coke and stayed with it until this day.

Not recognizing and respecting the necessary alignment of the three brains caused Coke millions of dollars worldwide.

Keeping this in mind, let's see how the mass neuro persuasion will strengthen you as a sales manager and help you and your whole department achieve better results.

FIVE PRINCIPLES OF MASS NEURO PERSUASION

1. Principle of Credibility Creation

Building and sustaining credibility with customers and crowds of customers is a factor of reputation, rapport and results.

$$\text{Credibility Creation} = \frac{\text{Reputation} + \text{Results} + \text{Rapport}}{\text{Self-Focus}}$$

Before the consumer buys into your product or service, they always do a lot of background checks. So building up your testimonials, social proof and certifications will give you and your team an edge. In the olden days, this was called word-of-mouth marketing. Today, it continues to influence reputation but with a huge added projection and magnifier called social media marketing.

Results and the quality performance of your product/service enhance credibility creation but good reputation and rapport in the marketplace will also drive your internal processes to consistently strive for better results.

the HeART of the CLOSE

2. Principle of Outward Focus

Go ahead and call it customer focus. That's okay! When large groups recognize that your company and your products are core-designed and core-produced to make their lives better, their romantic senses kick in and they flock to buy your products.

Companies like Tylenol and Toyota suffered serious setbacks in the outputs they had created a few decades ago. But because they rolled up their sleeves and jumped right into the mess to save the day, they kept the appreciation of the consumers.

Both these companies have had issues with the quality and performance of their products and both of them, have recalled and replaced their products, giving credence to their being outward customer focused. When your company and your sales team deliver with such an attitude, your marketplace will be moved to buy your products and to offer you their trust.

Outward focus is a two-way street with the first step mostly taken by the seller and the sales-agents. This principle of reciprocity of an organizational psyche is a function of its Romantic brain. Love me first, it says, and I will love you right back.

3. Principle of Differentiate Deliverables

Dove soap essentially caters to women so I have not used their products, but I have always admired this brand's approach and strategy.

Over a decade ago, Dove went radical and started a marketing promotion called "Campaign for real beauty". The campaign claimed to cater to real women; not the type who needed to conform to the generally accepted, visually appealing trend and culture of slim body types, fair complexions, and specific facial configurations. They created and marketed products for normal, everyday women of various shapes, sizes and physical challenges. Their move and mindset was so bold and so unique that the campaign brought them a tsunami of businesses from across the nations. To this day, Dove is looked up to for being different and yes, gutsy.

Train your people and your teams to stand apart and walk tall. It is value creation we're after; not hype. Our goal is to serve our customers well. It is not about keeping an eye on and becoming like the competition.

4. Principle of Emotional Anchoring

Just like an individual, large crowds can allow an idea or a mental synapse to bypass natural defensiveness and common sense. Whenever the Reactive brain of a large audience is impressed that your product is recognized and endorsed by their models of excellence or will serve a greater good, they rush to buy it en masse regardless of its quality and cost.

Lots of variables can trigger an emotional synapse in an individual. This usually occurs in the deeper recesses of the brain where feelings like fear, anger, doubt and compassion lie. Anything can stir up those neurons in the Reactive brain and spark it off in making a major buying decision, or not.

Companies can announce their products as locally made thus bringing pride and nationalism into the picture. Companies can announce that their products will go toward helping the needy or saving certain species of animals.

the HeART of the CLOSE

Companies can also claim shortages or price hikes to spark fear and drive people to buy.

A decade ago in India, McDonald's had a hard time breaking into the small-ethnic-restaurant market and its fear of eating food from a company that claimed to have served billions of burgers to the world. To Indians, burgers meant cows may have been killed to feed the world. McDonald's in India was definitely not serving pork or beef products but they couldn't bring in the crowds.

McDonald's then discovered that Indian movies and Indian movie stars have a huge impact on the country's mindset and belief system. They also learned that Indians love nostalgia and reminiscing. From these realizations, they created a campaign called "I'm loving it!"

For this campaign, McDonald's used vintage movie star look-alikes in a black and white audio-video campaign. Iconic stars like Dilip Kumar and Dev Anand were seen eating in a McDonald's classic style restaurant, biting into the vegetable burgers and claiming "I'm loving it!"

work in conjunction with your marketing team to equip your salespeople with creative ideas in your specific business

The campaign was a hit. It was funny and memorable and it reached into the hearts of the Indian masses. Now, a decade later, most McDonald's restaurants are packed to the rafters in India.

Work in conjunction with your marketing team to equip your

the HeART of the CLOSE

salespeople with creative ideas in your specific business, so they can drop these emotional anchors into the customer's mindset and improve performance and profits.

5. Principle of Sealing Deals with Silence

This principle works swimmingly well with individuals, and when its essence is applied to large groups it will bring similar results.

Example:

Right in the middle of a tough negotiation in the sales process (as explained under Negotiating Nuances in chapter 4) back away and ease off from pushing your customer. Let his three brains go to work with each other. This is risky but if you have played all of your earlier cards right then you are bound to trump.

For larger groups and organizations, silence works by creating and sustaining an environment where you provide everything your prospective client needs to envision a solution and enable him to act and make the right choice. Thus, your job as a marketer/salesperson is to orchestrate the setting and the ambiance such that the action of your prospective client having it their way ends up in your favor.

Many successful online media companies have become giants because they created the environment for the clients to design and use their products according to the will of these clients, but the actual encashing of money happens in the giant online seller's bank.

These five principles behind the neuropsychology of large groups

the HeART of the CLOSE

of people will help create the appropriate sales strategies and will lead your team profitably.

TWO: ALIGNING ENTERPRISE STRATEGY AND SALES TEAM PLANS

Let's just say that any business or company offering products and services in the marketplace is an enterprise, and they do it for profit. Some claim they don't work for a profit. So be it. But they do work for non-tangible, emotional, spiritual gains and they need revenue, funds, and cash to be able to continue doing what they do. Thus, every organization is an enterprise.

Now there are simple enterprises like Ben & Jerry's ice cream, and then there are complex enterprises like Google, whose revenue generation processes only a few people know about or understand.

Now, let's cut up all enterprises into three sections. (1) Product development and management; (2) Brand promotion and delivery, and (3) Customer relationship and management. The canvas where these three sections rest and intertwine is Sales and Service. Not having sales means no customers; not having customers means no product development and no product. Not having customers will lead to the demise of the brand and the business.

In juggling the needs of these three sections, the sales and service cannot afford to let any of them down. Otherwise, in time, the enterprise will die.

In tandem with this process is the recognition of the fact that

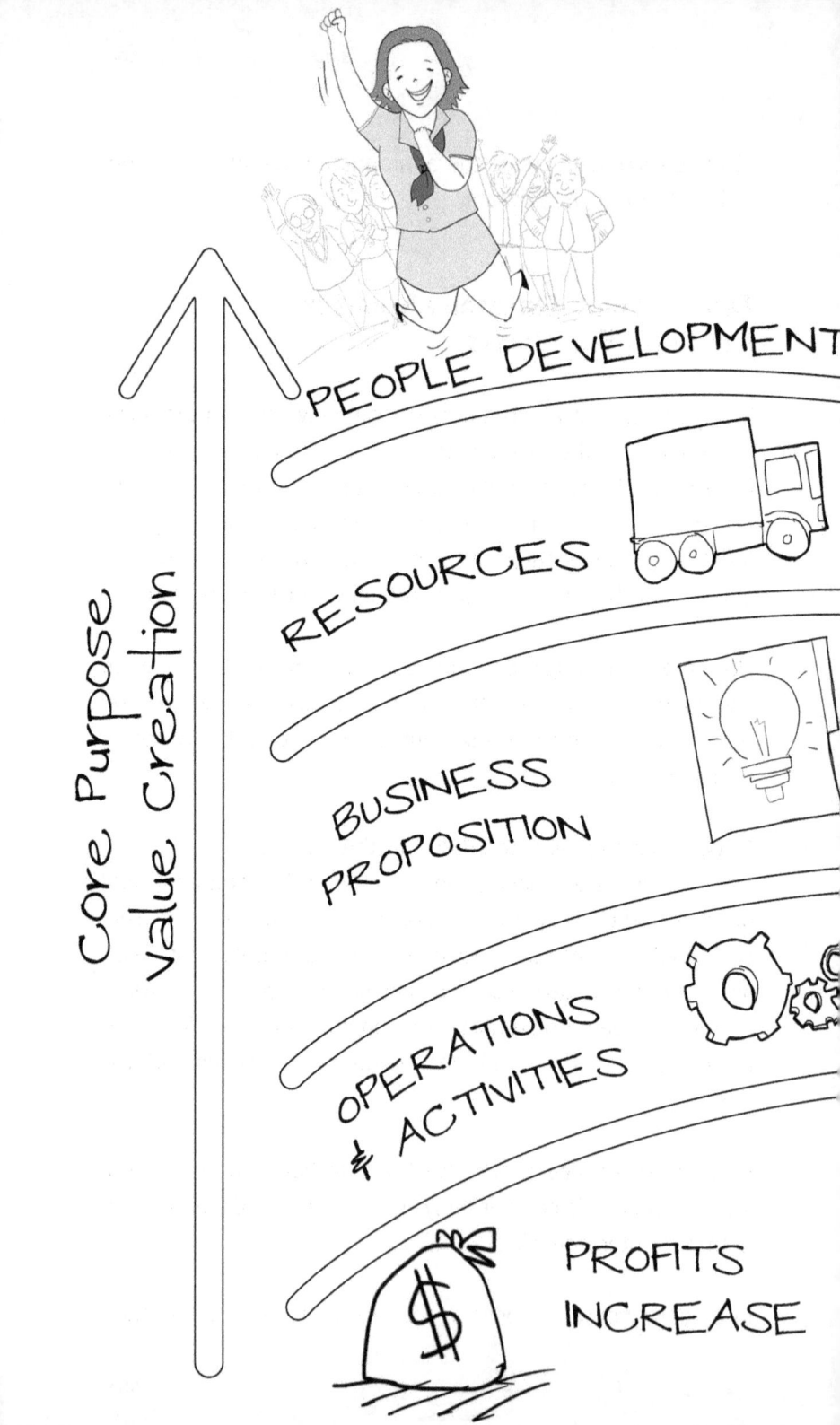

all enterprises must earn, evolve, and grow continuously. That, essentially, is the desired core purpose of any enterprise. Serving people, planet, and profits is a by-product of this core purpose to learn, evolve, and grow.

Sales and service is the key factor to an enterprise being able to live up to its core desired purpose. Thus, in aligning the sales department with the core-desired purpose of the enterprise, all sales plans must include these components.

Components of a Sales Plan
- Alignment and resonance with all other departments;
- Support of existing structure, systems, and procedures to keep the value flowing from production to consumption;
- Assessment and forecasting of how much production needs to be done, how to be cost-efficient in delivering the brand promise, how many additional customers to take and then have the capability to level-up in a given period.

Forecasting and planning resources is not the most obvious task of the sales department. Communication channels need to be well greased and feedback flow must be continuous and consistent for the sales department's forecasting and planning to effectively support the enterprise's progress.

Beliefs, Behaviors and Business Results

A manager-leader's job is to pay attention to details as well as to value the big-picture strategy of the business.

The 4 cogs of an enterprise are profits, processes, promotions, and its people.

the HeART of the CLOSE

In partnership with other department heads, your job as sales manager is to ensure all cogs or wheels are tuned, aligned and move in harmony. This is achieved when the departments support each other. It's true that as sales

Your business outcomes are the results of how your sales team members behave.

manager your focus is on sales promotions and profits but you also need to back up the managers and staff who are handling the processes.

Your business outcomes are the results of how your sales team members behave. How they behave is driven by what they believe. Your job is to show them a big-picture vision they can focus on and thus, improve behaviour and business results.

THREE: MANAGING TERRITORIES, MANAGING PEOPLE

Every marketplace, regardless of how it is laid out, can be cut up in many different ways. The manner in which a manager cuts up territories and assigns his people is based on the company's business model and strategy. It is also based on the intentions and perceptions of the sales manager.

Let's say you are a property sales agency representing multiple developers in a single state of 15,000 square meters and with a population density of 7.5 million people. Let's suppose you manage 50 incentivized salespeople. Now further suppose that your target clientele make up only 0.2% of that population, which would be about 15,000 potential customers. How would you cut up this pie to assign among your 50 sales people?

You can divide and assign territories in any of the 5 ways below:

- By just dividing in equal numbers;
- By income levels and by net worth, if you can get such data;
- By reach and physical accessibility from your location and point of reference;
- By the past performance of the client; or
- By the salespeople's experience and capabilities.

Regardless of how you segment the market and cut up this territory, you must understand that the market and other conditions will always be in a state of flux. New competition may enter your territories. Your salespeople may move on and new ones will move in.

Strategies to manage market conditions and staff turnover

- You could consider to first focus proactively on the primary, easy-to-reach, easy-to- teach, and easy-to-close customers.
- Next, consider responding to your secondary and your tertiary markets based on needs. This means you only respond to them if they reach out to you or if they are referred to you.
- Thirdly and to avoid discord and conflict in your team, assign high performers and competent salespeople to primary accounts and let newcomers work up the ladder through the secondary and tertiary markets.

Managing territories and people in sales management is a tricky and highly sensitive numbers-and-performance game. You will need to call on all the information you know about the

the HeART of the CLOSE

Reasoning, the Romantic, and the Reactive brains to make the most out of your team, your existing resources and your clients.

A SALES MANAGER'S MAJOR TASKS IN MANAGING PEOPLE:

1. Delegating with precision

All conversations generally are and must be a two-way democratic street. Sometimes, however, you, as sales manager, will need to give marching orders to your troops.

Three Steps to Effective Delegation recommended by *the HeART of the CLOSE*:

a. Choose the right person for the right job. Check that the task you assign is not too heavy or too light for the shoulders of the troopers. If you overburden an individual, it will have negative impact on her other responsibilities and stunt her growth. If you assign a task that is too light to a highly capable, competent person then she will take it lightly, will not be sufficiently challenged and will not grow. When assigning the right job to the right person, make sure she has the tools and resources to enable her to do the job.

b. State the task precisely without being either too brief or too verbose. Think through the job and the job description and then place yourself in their shoes before you describe what needs to be done. In addition to being clear and concise about what needs to be done, make sure the intended result is crystallized in numbers. The outcome needs to be measurable. Like good goal setting, delegating needs specificity and measurability.

On the other hand, give them room to manoeuvre and play when creating the results. Refrain from breathing down their necks while they execute the job. It's called empowerment.

c. Lastly, provide a framework and timeline for your troops to be able to communicate and track their own progress. Be firm on timelines and reporting methods and be open and accessible for clarification and support.

Learning to delegate assignments and tasks is a fine skill. As you become better at this, your job gets easier. You progress as a manager and your team members develop into more competent salespeople.

It is wise to remember that delegating with clarity will be appreciated by the Reasoning brain; providing context will appeal to the Romantic brain; and empowering with space to manoeuvre will keep Reactive brain from responding or resisting out of fear and anger.

2. Handling Conflict and Building Teams

It takes time for people to learn to trust, come together and become a productive team. This is particularly true in the field of sales which (together with the Marketing Team) is the face and front of every enterprise and where growth and income are directly correlated to performance.

Discord among sales-agents is minimized if your systems and structures are in place. If your team has been together through shared successes and failures, the trust levels will be high and conflict will likewise decrease.

the HeART of the CLOSE

I have come across managers who handle conflict between two or more sales personnel simply by calling them in for a private meeting and letting them go at each other. These managers hope that their own presence and attempts at intervention will resolve conflict and bring about peace. This does not happen easily.

I have witnessed scores of team building sessions where facilitators introduce a trust game, bring in conflict issues and expect people to kiss and make up. This does not happen, at least not in the deeper emotional levels. In such scenarios, the Reasoning brain puts on an act of compromise and forms a pact with the Reactive brain to plot revenge sometime in the future.

Recommendations for handling conflict:

a. Dig up all data and hearsay about the conflict issue. Gather only the data and hold yourself back from making judgments.

b. Have a private conversation with each of the involved parties. Again, gather only data. Refrain from coming to conclusions.

c. After gathering all facts and listening to the feelings from all sides, brainstorm on your own or with neutral colleagues for ideas on resolving the issue.

d. If you have the time and resources, have one more conversation in private with each of the involved parties. Here, you will discover that from the time of your first conversation with them, their Reasoning, Romantic, and Reactive brains have done some private thinking and reflecting. You will, with patience, learn that people are generally keen and open to resolving conflict and moving on.

e. Employ empathy to stay focused on finding healing and a lasting solution to the issue rather than just a remedy or a working compromise.

After you've had positive and solution-focused conversations with the individual parties and have had them anchor those ideas down, then it is time to bring the parties together. A resolution can more easily be achieved.

Handling conflict and being an affiliative leader is a truly important skill set for a sales manager.

Responsibilities and Rewards

Thousands of researches and studies have been done about what keeps people engaged, empowered and productive. In his book Drive, Daniel Pink claims that a proper dose of freedom to experiment at work, continuous improvement of a chosen craft and a focus towards a higher purpose keep people driven and productive. He calls it autonomy, mastery and purpose at work and life.

Abraham Maslow, in his popular 1943 study of human developmental needs, postulates that human motivation moves across physiological, safety, emotional, status and self-actualization needs.

What these translate to for the sales profession is, depending on their life conditions and the output they create, people can be motivated by tangible incentives at times and by non-tangible

ones at other times. Most of us are constantly clamouring up and down this theoretical pyramid of human developmental needs. Sometimes physical needs satisfy us, sometimes it's emotional needs, and at other times, it's spiritual.

A friend of mine who worked in an insurance firm once related how for three years in a row, their star-rated salesperson was awarded with cash and a large plaque of appreciation at their annual sales rally. Despite the increase in the incentive and the size of the plaque, his performance began to dwindle, year-on-year.

The perplexed sales director, in consultation with the CEO, decided to change tactics. They did some research and discovered that he deeply loved nurturing his twin teenage daughters. On the following year, unbeknownst to the salesperson, his manager got hold of a beautiful photograph of his twin daughters. He had it converted into a watercolour painting and had it beautifully framed. At the annual awards, in the presence of thousands of his colleagues, the sales manager presented this award to his salesperson. For many months after that event the star salesperson stayed fired up and delivered exceedingly brilliant results. The strategy worked.

On another occasion there was this retired businessman who lived in a neighbourhood where children would play outside his window and make a huge racket. He consulted neighbours and friends on how to drive the kids to go play somewhere else but none could give him a creative idea. Being a former entrepreneur, he approached the kids and, for a week, offered them a dollar for every hour they played and made a racket in front of his house. On the following week, he dropped the incentive from a dollar an hour to 50 cents an hour of screaming and shouting.

On the third week he begged to drop the rate to 25 cents an hour for the same cacophony and chaos. The kids thought this was humiliating and backed out. They called it "no deal!" and soon, moved into another part of the neighbourhood where their noise-making skills would be more appreciated.

When managing sales teams of varying skill levels with differing goals and timelines, a manager needs to combine the elements of material incentives, of freedom and of self-actualization in such a way so the players can work at optimum levels and learn to align the external goals

A creative sales manager needs to juggle ideas and applications on the outside in such a way so the whirring and shifting gears among the Reasoning, Romantic and the Reactive brains of his team members.

with their internal motivations. Sometimes, managers need to increase responsibilities and match them with privileges. At other times, rewards need to be added or decreased as an agreed consequence. In effect a creative sales manager needs to juggle ideas and applications on the outside in such a way so the whirring and shifting gears among the Reasoning, Romantic and the Reactive brains of his team members reach an optimum level and becomes self-sustaining.

FOUR: MANAGING TIME AND ALLOCATING RESOURCES

Being sales manager is a real "management" juggle. Like a good general, you need to raise your perspective and view the lay of the land. You have multiple products and services with a variety of prices and proposals to juggle with. Your targets are mostly moving and other people are simultaneously chasing the same targets. You have quotas, reports, bosses and the entire enterprise growth to deal with. Finally, you often lead a motley group of salespeople of different calibres and range.

In its most basic form, your sales management quadrant is made up of products, pricing, people and customers juxtaposed against the only two currencies we have to deal with, time and money.

How you mix, match and maximize these resources will depend on your products, niche, business conditions, needs and strategic goals. No single rule of thumb works in winning this war but listed below are five basic tactics.

1. Assign senior salespeople to the challenging customers. This could initially cost you more.
2. Assign junior salespeople to take on slow-moving products. This will use up more time and money but will simultaneously train and hone these salespeople.
3. Innovate and improve products. This may raise your costs and lower margins but will raise consumer interest in the product.
4. Lower prices which will, however, correspondingly decrease profits.
5. Or, observe market conditions and then launch products or people into it.

the HeART of the CLOSE

The best strategies are those that have worked in the past and are applicable in the ever- changing market and economic conditions. Speed, accuracy and adaptability are key components when executing plans.

FIVE: INSPIRING YOUR TEAMS

Overlaps exist among teaching, training, mentoring, counselling and coaching. The same is true with inspiring, motivating, influencing, and preaching.

Motivating is when there is something measurable to gain, either tangible or non-tangible. It is only when others are internally motivated that we can come close to inspiring our teams. Influencing is when a manager orchestrates work-life circumstances for another to encourage that person to make a decision for himself in the direction which the manager had in mind. Preaching is when you propose a higher, more profound authority to direct the team, and many times, that higher authority is you, the sales manager. These three approaches have their pros and cons.

True leaders generally lean toward inspiring others. What exactly is inspiring and how does a sales leader inspire others? When we peep into the etymology of the word, inspiration is about lighting a fire in the spirit of an individual. This is the same as getting all the three brains lined up and focused on a specific goal, a single dream, and a singular intention.

True leaders generally lean toward inspiring others.

A salesperson gets inspired by

the HeART of the CLOSE

either a role model or a distant ideal that lays hidden within her. So how does a sales leader spark off this fire? Consider these elements.

1. Become a role model. Sales leaders can inspire others when they are living and performing at their fullest potential, when their beliefs, attitudes, behaviour and therefore, the outcomes too, are congruent and ecologic.

2. Acquire long-term credibility. Credibility comes from a combination of personal competencies, reliability and capability to consistently take on new responsibilities. Team members get inspired when the sales manager is someone they can approach for knowledge and guidance, who performs competently, and who supportively stands by them. Creating this solid image becomes a strong personal brand and a powerful source of inspiration.

3. Balance vision and reality. A sales leader can inspire when he acknowledges reality while he also unearths strengths, thus, eliciting optimism from the team as they look toward a brighter horizon. In this third element, you will have to master powerful speaking and communicating skills. You will need to understand how your message's substance and structure and your speaking style come together to potently work through your team's three brains to touch their hearts and move their minds.

I remember a rough patch of years when business had really dropped for me. My sales were down to a crawl partly because the trade winds favoured China at that time. I was disappointed and quickly losing motivation. My friend Sidney Schindler said, "Raju you are trying to leap out of a hole and beat the odds at once. It doesn't work that way in life. You've got to carefully climb out…one order at a time. Remember, inch by inch it's a cinch and yard by yard it is very hard." This made me smile and I haven't forgotten his wise and inspiring words since.

These three elements can be innate in a leader but more often, they are choices made and habits built by strengthening the partnership between the Reasoning and the Romantic Brains. The former makes the choice and sustains the discipline while the latter keeps the hope alive and the eye on the distant, bigger picture. Optimising the partnership between the brains requires will, discipline and lots of practice so take every opportunity to inspire. Stand and speak up, then take feedback on how you got to touch hearts, move minds and fire up spirits. Do this often. Do this repeatedly. Soon your intentions and actions will clearly and powerfully inspire others.

the HeART of the CLOSE

CHAPTER 6

COACHING, DEVELOPING OTHERS

Let's start by talking about what coaching is not. Coaching is not telling. It is not teaching, not training, and not even mentoring. When you tell something to someone, you deliver sound and the listener probably hears it. Does he accept, understand, and act upon it? Only he will know and only he can say.

Coaching is not teaching. Teaching is when your listener doesn't know the subject or the skill at hand as well as you do, and so you explain and maybe demonstrate. In this case you need to know the subject at hand much better and deeper than your listener or student.

Coaching is not training. Training is when you facilitate the learning of a skill; say biking or using Microsoft Excel. You can be referred to as a "coach" but you're not truly coaching in the real sense.

Coaching is not mentoring. Mentor is the name of a man in whose care Telemachus, the son of King Ulysses of Ithaca was put under. Ulysses (also known as Odysseus in Greek) asked Mentor to look after his son when he went off to fight the legendary Trojan Wars which lasted 20 years. Apparently, Mentor did such a good job of caring for Telemachus that the word "mentor" moved into the language as the name for a person who teaches principles and practices to his ward and pupil. Thus, you mentor someone also when you are better than him in specific subjects and skills.

To be a coach or to coach someone, you do not have to necessarily be better than the person you are coaching in that specific skill set. To coach is to evoke and to facilitate the unlocking of innate potential in the person you are coaching.

A coach helps you set goals and then stands back and watches as you execute and achieve them.

The professions that come closest to coaching might be a combination of doctor, counsellor, and guide. Yet these three are not quite coaching because they somehow prescribe and indoctrinate.

Coaching provides context but no content. Coaching provides the framework but doesn't provide any principles to the one being coached. Coaching only challenges assumptions, unearths desires and strengths and then maybe co-designs a strategy to achieve those desires and optimize those strengths. A coach helps you set goals and then stands back and watches as you execute and achieve them. Thousands of definitions of

the HeART of the CLOSE

coaching exist along with thousands of principles for practicing coaching.

To establish a clear understanding of coaching let me, again take you back a few hundred years in time to Italy and modern day Rome.

In Florence, Italy, a young sculptor was commissioned to do a statue of a well-loved Biblical character out of a discarded Carrara marble piece. It was a project nobody wanted to be part of. Many other sculptors said the piece of marble was rotten, porous and scarred. None of them wanted to be associated with such work lest their names and honor be tainted.

Young Michelangelo, as he approached and surveyed the stained and scarred rock, paid little attention to the rumours or the damaged external conditions of the rock. His eyes and his heart saw only the beauty and elegance lying hidden within the rock. He imagined what the rock could become when all the unnecessary parts were chipped away by his skilled and caring hands.

He had the rock brought to his studio and began chipping away it. After many days and nights of labouring with love and polishing off the unnecessary bits from the rock, artist Michelangelo succeeded in unearthing and bringing to life the amazingly beautiful statue of David. It still stands tall and proud at the Galleria dell' Accademia as an homage to an artist -a coach who saw beauty, brilliance and potential in a piece of discarded rock.

Such is the heart of coaching. It is the art and science of seeing something powerful inside another person and then carefully, lovingly and scientifically releasing and unleashing that potential. To be a coach is to be an awakener of sorts. To be a coach is to be an almost invisible, non-interfering guide by the side. That's what coaching is.

In this 6th chapter, **the HeART of the CLOSE** will briefly discuss the business benefits of coaching and will then lay down a five-step process for unleashing the power and potential hidden inside your sales personnel.

RATIONALE AND BENEFITS OF COACHING

Three reasons for every sales manager to place coaching on top of his developmental priorities are:

1. Coaching unleashes Individual and Team excellence.

Most people, including salespeople, usually perform and deliver below their potential. It is a human malady. The fear that lurks in our Reactive Brain incapacitates and corrodes the passion and the strengths that reside in our beings. It is as if our strengths, skills and hopes get submerged under an unconscious ocean of doubt and mediocrity.

Coaching helps unearth these strengths. It wipes away our fears and fires up our spirits to hope, to plan, and to execute in a highly focused, smoothly flowing way as we move with passion toward a productive future.

When individuals gain internal alignment, their ability to absorb, ideate, analyse and communicate improves and they perform at optimal levels. They learn to rapidly build rapport to acquire and sustain deeper trust. Team members who have high levels of trust and rapport and who are able to articulate ideas and create buy-ins from others are always an asset to the organization.

2. Coaching helps enterprises achieve breakthroughs.

All businesses go through good and tough times. Businesses that manage to walk through such rough patches are able to do so because they are focused and flexible, and because all of their functional parts move and work like a well-designed machine.

American management consultant, educator, and author Peter F. Drucker once claimed all successful businesses necessarily perform two major actions: they innovate and they market. Businesses innovate on products, services, processes, and projects. They market the same stuff: products, services, processes, and projects. Now this marketing is done not just externally but also towards the internal customer.

Coaching supports this constant process of innovating and marketing breakthroughs by accomplishing the following:

- **Knowledge Transfer:** Over time every enterprise acquires, adopts, and generates knowledge just like a living system. With coaching, managers and leaders can constantly transfer and diffuse this dynamic knowledge throughout the whole enterprise.

- **Succession planning:** Beyond psychometric tools and performance reports, the personalized element

the HeART of the CLOSE

of coaching helps an organization in selecting and grooming high potential employees and salespeople to take up leadership positions. Coaching can also do some fine tuning and pruning until they become the best leaders they can be.

3. Coaching directly impacts bottom lines.

Companies can claim to be the best at this or an expert at that. They can claim to be number one in this segment and top performer in that area. But what truly measures business performance is how much money they make year after year and how well they keep up their capabilities and capacities to consistently deliver better financial results year after year.

It matters little whether you are a not-for-profit or a socio civic organization. What matters beyond the good service that an organisation provides is for money to flow regularly and abundantly in that organization.

Coaching holds the key in sustaining the flow of money through the veins of every enterprise.

Revisiting the HeART of the CLOSE Concepts

Before **the HeART of the CLOSE** takes you through the coaching process, it is important to revisit some of the concepts discussed in the preceding chapters of this book because the coaching process is not a stand-alone process. Coaching is a conversation and an interaction. Like selling, coaching also necessitates that the coach is grounded and thoroughly knows his role so that he can uncover the needs and wants of the person he is coaching.

The sections that require revisiting and reviewing are as follows:

1. The Reasoning, Romantic, and the Reactive Brains in chapter 1
2. Intention is the Driver in chapter 2
3. Only Action is Measurable in chapter 2
4. Sensory Acuity Enhanced Awareness in chapter 3
5. Finding Quiet Ground in chapter 3
6. Managing Perceptual Positions in chapter 3
7. The Five I's of Mindful Listening in chapter 3
8. Recognition and Respect for Diversity and Change in chapter 3
9. The 5R Questioning Toolbox in chapter 3
10. SMARTer Goal Setting in chapter 5
11. Inspiring the Teams in chapter 5

Reviewing these sections will now be easier since you have already studied them previously. The most relevant among the 11 recommended sections are The Five I's of Listening, the 5R Questioning Toolbox and Finding Quiet Ground.

FIVE PHASES OF THE COACHING PROCESS

Phase ONE: ENVISION SUCCESS

Whenever you take up the assignment of coaching a salesperson, it is necessary that you personally see the salesperson's potential. If you do not see and believe this, then you will get nowhere with this salesperson. It is like trying to launch an arrow from a bow with broken strings. When you agree to coach someone, you must envision success. When an individual approaches you to seek such support, that specific action of her wanting to be coached comes from her powerful intentions to learn,

grow and perform well. In the coaching world, this is known as coaching receptivity. That means they have the desire and thus they become coachable.

When you and your salesperson get together, your first conversations should be about the possibilities, followed by an articulation and description of the necessary attitude/mindset adjustments to enable her to do things differently and improve her performance.

Steps for Envisioning Success:

a. **Meet the standards.** Make sure you are a qualified coach, who is competent and knowledgeable. This does not mean you must be a better salesperson. It means you need to know how to coach.

b. **Get an agreement.** In the coaching profession which also includes life coaching (outside the sales team or business organization) getting into a coaching relationship means making an agreement. Within an organization and the sales team where you are the manager, an understanding will suffice as an agreement. Setting an agreement is getting your salesperson to commit to her growth.

c. **Build trust.** At this phase of Envisioning Success, it is crucial for your salesperson to believe and observe, from your behaviour, that her growth is your first priority; not your team goals and most definitely not an agenda of your egoistical satisfaction.

d. **Be Present.** This is needed not just in this first phase but throughout the coaching process. On every encounter you need to be fully present and give full attention. It will not work if you do coaching sessions while staring at your computer screen or working your way through a full day's work load. That is totally unacceptable for a coach. You have to be present–mind, body, soul and laptop¬– for your salesperson. Applying the 5I's of listening from Chapter 3 will help you do that.

Phase TWO: ENUMERATE RESOURCES

After gaining the trust of your salesperson, this second phase is when you start diving in to pull out the pearls of wisdom, strength and confidence from her mind, body, and soul.

From her words and her stories, listen deeply for the emotional and intellectual resources she possesses. Listen in for expressions of strengths and hopes and note these resources down. These are the resources you will be using to enable and empower her. The 5-R questioning toolbox will help you do this effectively and powerfully.

Use gentle, positive questions to explore and understand not just the big picture but also the nuances of her personality, interpersonal style and self-expectations. Listen to her stories with full attention. Smile, nod and encourage her to go on and tell you more. Revealing more demonstrates her increasing trust in you

Use gentle, positive questions to explore and understand not just the big picture but also the nuances of her personality, interpersonal style and self expectations

the HeART of the CLOSE

and helps you identify the resources to create a strategy of improvement and success for her. At this phase:

- Discover and list what you both believe are her strengths.
- Highlight past successes with similar endeavours.
- List material, emotional and social resources that she can tap.

Phase THREE: ENGINEER THE PROCESS

From the first two phases, you will accumulate answers to questions like:

- How are things at work?
- How do you monitor the accounts you are tracing?
- What can be improved, expedited in the sales cycle?
- What are examples of your past successes with a client such as the one you are chasing?
- What exactly do you want to happen? What exactly do you want to create?

In this phase of Engineering the Process towards growth and success, you, as coach, will perform three actions, in conversation with the salesperson.

a. Speak Directly to the Salesperson

Speak to your salesperson directly and in the present tense, using "I" and "you," (instead of "she, he or them.") Be kind and empathetic but firm and clear.

Create awareness of what he has been doing so far. In his consciousness raise the attitudes and habits that will bring about improvement in performance. This could range from adjusting his mindset, fulfilling commitments and managing time to knowing more about the product and understanding customer needs. Bring up the changes that need to be done and set the specific challenge on the desktop of his Reasoning, Romantic, and Reactive brains. All three will need to tackle the issue at hand.

Use tact and skill so your salesperson not only acknowledges the challenge but also verbalizes it himself in his own words and with conviction. When your salesperson, with your gentle questioning, realizes and sees the light and wisdom, then half of your coaching work is done. You have reached the point when the salesperson is ready to commit toward transformation and change. This is a good time to patiently and gently let the salesperson set up various performance goals.

b.   Set Goals and Seek Accountability.

As a sales manager/coach, you have several objectives for coaching your salesperson. Two major objectives are firstly, to develop your sales personnel and secondly, to reach your team's sales targets. Coaching in and of itself should have only the pure agenda of developing your salesperson. But as a sales manager you must also seek results that are team-and-enterprise-oriented. Thus, when your salesperson sets his personal goals it is incumbent upon you to chase them and seek accountability because this will, directly and indirectly, impact on you and the entire team's performance.

During this goal setting phase, it is best to refer back to SMARTer Goal Setting in chapter 5.

Remember the following:
- Be clear about what is to be achieved.
- Be specific about how this will be measured: in calls per

the HeART of the CLOSE

day, closes per week or total dollar sales per month.

- Be precise about when and how the salesperson must report to you.

Examples of personal goals your salesperson can set for himself:

- Perform more calls per day
- Make more receipts per week
- Send out more proposals within a given period.
- Speed up reportorial work. (Sales reports on calls made, proposals sent, meetings held, etc.)
- Work in tandem with the technical/production departments, etc.
- If used, systematize, structure and keep all kinds of business software functioning well in the enterprise.
- Prepare charts showing progress per account, per product, per category, even per territory per month.

Simultaneous to coaching your salesperson toward achieving his personal goals, you also need to have on the desktop of your mind and on our office walls, the sales figures per territory, per account, per product and per salesperson.

Thus, switching hats from gentle, supportive coach to number-savvy, results-oriented head of the sales department is what makes being a sales manager a daunting role.

c. Provide Feedback, Appreciatively

The toughest task of any manager-leader is breaking bad news and doing it in a benign and productive way. The day you master how to provide constructive and corrective feedback without drawing blood is the day you can claim to have touched the shores of leadership wisdom.

the HeART of the CLOSE

Feedback may appear hard on the surface but is actually supportive, corrective and developmental at the core. These five simple attitude and behaviour practices for providing feedback will highlight the developmental benefits at the core.

- View the dropping performance or the floor behaviour as an event. Do not look at it as something good or bad, but simply as an "event" in a day in the life of a salesperson and sales manager.

- Refrain from getting emotional, from taking it personally or from becoming personally attached to the outcomes. Practice Managing Perceptual Positions as described in chapter 3.

- Manage your demeanour and the restlessness of your Reactive Brain, which tends to show its fangs every now and then. Juggle the thoughts, ideas, and opinions about the incident between your Reasoning and the Romantic Brain to calm and cool down your Reactive Brain.

- Describe the incident to the salesperson by stating it objectively and in the simplest possible terms. Don't say "I think" "I believe", "I guess", "I assume". Just state the situation and describe what you saw. Wait for your salesperson to respond. It is possible that upon sensing your equanimity, she will take responsibility, suggest solutions and even offer to work on it herself. If this happens, it can be the end of the feedback session because your salesperson has taken responsibility and there is no need to establish accountability or to correct.
  Share what you felt over the incident only when your salesperson responds and acknowledges the change that

the HeART of the CLOSE

needs to come about.

- Explain the "why and the how" or the benefits that could come about from any recommendations you give. Acknowledge, accept and understand the challenge at hand. Finally, end your feedback in a warm and friendly manner.

Many years ago I read a book entitled True Freedom written by an Australian monk living in Thailand. He wrote about a day when he was extremely mad at a junior monk for having messed up on a project. He sent for the monk and had planned to give him a tongue lashing to remember. As he sat there fuming, he realized he did not like the "state" he had driven himself into! Soon he began to think of the many years he had known the junior monk. He remembered the times they had laughed together at other failures and successes. He remembered the times they had struggled and survived through tough periods. A smile slowly came upon his face just at the time when the junior monk knocked at his door and asked to be let in.

You can guess pretty well how that planned tongue lashing went. At the end of 20 minutes, after they brainstormed ideas and action plans, they parted ways laughingly and with hearts and minds filled with new vigour and hope.

So, whenever you get mad or upset at any of your salespersons' performance, look back at their track record, look back at your relationship and from that perspective, slowly and gently speak up. Thus, the rule of thumb in providing corrective feedback appreciatively is to see the big picture, remove your ego from the equation and mutually find a way forward into growth and success.

Phase FOUR: EMPOWER AND ENERGIZE

In the late 80's in New York, my friend and mentor, Sidney Schindler, sometimes accompanied me on sales calls. Sidney was a sales veteran and a humongously charming person to be around. People flocked to him and struck up conversations with him. When he offered information and tips, they trusted his words and his wisdom.

Between the two of us, Sidney was much more knowledgeable, experienced and empowered to give concessions and close deals. But on our sales calls to potential customer, Sidney never openly demonstrated that fact. He performed the introductions and then he took the back seat, speaking up only as and when I turned to him for help. Never during a sales call did he present himself as a senior partner or tried to impress me or the customer with his communication skills.

He did talk to me when we had walked a block or two from the client's office. And, when he talked, it was never about his opinions or what he thought was right. It was always about what I, the salesperson thought went well, and what I could do better the next time around. He backed up whatever observations and ideas I expressed and cheered me on.

On the rare occasions Sidney gave me a tip or two, they never seemed like tips. They always seemed like ideas and opinions we had both generated while chatting about the business at hand. He was cool, calm, stylish, and never imposed himself upon me as a mentor or a coach. Sidney Schindler has now moved on to a better place but he has left me a treasure trove of wisdom and insights on how to draw the best from people.

the HeART of the CLOSE

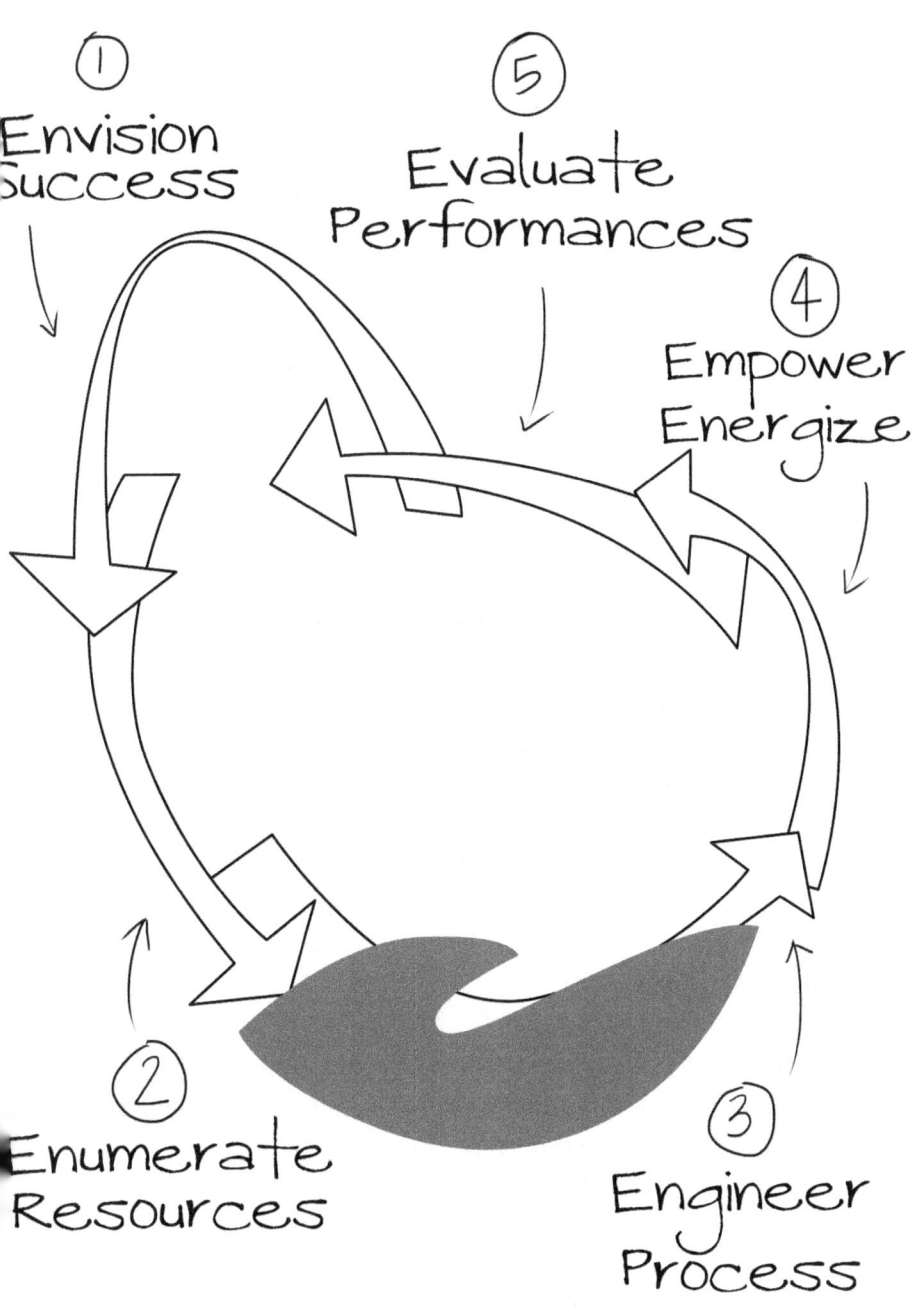

① Envision
Success

⑤ Evaluate
Performances

④ Empower
Energize

② Enumerate
Resources

③ Engineer
Process

Whether you do it in the office or in the field, always choose to coach by consistently energizing and empowering your salespeople in a quiet, mostly invisible manner. Your glory as a manager-coach will come when your salespeople feel they have achieved all their objectives on their own

Evoke breakthroughs

"You are only as good as your last performance."

"Nothing succeeds like success!"

"The only person you need to compete against is yourself"

Clichés these all may be, but clichés often carry age-old wisdom.

No matter how well your salesperson or sales team is doing, your job as a sales manager/performance coach is to have them continuously raising the bar on themselves. Failure in any profession can get you down and keep you there. It is all the more magnified in the selling profession where your job description and its accompanying challenges often take on a new scope based on customer needs, market demands, and internal changes.

Your job is to keep your salesperson's mind, body and spirit in top shape at all times. Your efforts at externally developing, nurturing and cheering must seep through her needs and the internal fancies of her Reasoning, Romantic and especially, her Reactive Brain.

Steps you can take with your salesperson to improve her work performance and consistently achieve breakthrough results are:

the HeART of the CLOSE

- Be available and open.
- Challenge their minds often.
- Re-align focus on distant goals, whether they are personal or professional.
- Highlight parallels between their personal values and corporate values.

Your job is to keep your salesperson's mind, body and spirit in top shape at all times.

- Stand by them, supportively and quietly during their tough times.
- Cheer them on when they are in the flow and striking gold.
- Celebrate unabashedly and authentically together when they succeed.

Phase FIVE: EVALUATE PERFORMANCES

As a sales coach your job is to establish accountability and celebrate success in goals set up by your salesperson for herself. As a sales manager your job requires that you generate results for your department as well as revenue for the whole enterprise.

The metrics of both the salesperson's and your team's performance can be based on and drawn from the Heart of the Close sales process, specifically from the Stages of the Seller Side Heart in chapter 4, namely.

a. **Connect with clarity.**

This connection may be a phone call, an email or a face-to-face meet up. You can measure and rank the effectiveness, the precision and the drawing-in quality of the interaction. You may also count the number of leads converted into opportunities by every salesperson.

b. Engage creatively and ethically.

As these connections get be converted into opportunities. You can monitor how long and how well the salesperson sustains the relationship. Has a client begun to trust and offer information? You can count and rank the quality of needs and wants discovered and the time taken to get to this point in the sales cycle.

Most products and services have industry-standard, turn-around times on the sales cycle, better known as customer traction time. You can measure an individual's performance by industry-standards or by your own business standards.

c. Influence and convert conscientiously.

This is the stage where your salesperson is in the middle of or about to present solutions to the customer. At this point, you can measure how many of your clients start talking about time, money, terms, warranties, and other business details.

You will remember from chapter 4 that this stage is not yet the closing stage. There will be negotiations. Even after you close, you cannot yet realistically call it a close. But you can track the number or percentage of clients who have come to the table with the intention to negotiate and then buy.

d. Acquire authentic commitment.

This is the easiest to measure based on (i) Number of contracts signed; (ii) Total number of dollars sold over a period of time; and (iii) time taken to achieve those figures in comparison to last year's performance and in alignment with this year's sales plan.

Sales Control	Connect with Clarity	Engage	Influence	Acquire	Serve
Person 1					
Person 2					
Person 3					
Person 4					
Person 5					

e. Serve wholeheartedly.

Create a policy and measure performance against the following:
- How long does the salesperson stay involved after the sale is concluded?
- How smooth and easy is it for the Legal, Billing, and other after-sales departments to take over the new contract?
- Does the salesperson pick up new leads and new referrals?
- Does he keep the doors open for new business from the same client?
- Does the customer stay keen on working with the salesperson for other needs?

Whichever criteria or units of measure you use throughout the process, make sure there is a person or a team assigned to consistently track and update the results. Doing so will help you focus and plan at what capacity you can take on new frontiers for your department and the whole enterprise.

CHAPTER 6

SELLING, TOMORROW

It would be nicely satisfying if I could claim that ***the HeART of the CLOSE*** is the cutting-edge knowledge and technology about social interaction and selling. But I know I cannot and I will not even attempt to make such a claim.

Leaders and anthropologists have asserted that in the last 20 years, humankind and civilization has seen so much more developments and innovations in comparison to what they have witnessed over the earlier 200 years.

Today, with just the click of a few buttons on our tablets and mobile devices, we can access not just information but knowledge and even great wisdom directly from its authors and original source. We are able to check our pulse, know our blood pressure, learn about traffic conditions in a city 10,000 miles away, make business decisions and even transfer millions of dollars with e easy taps on a silicon screen.

the HeART of the CLOSE

Has this all impacted how we buy and sell products and services? Yes, in many ways. Will this all change a lot more in the coming days and years? Oh yes. The signs are screaming into our faces.

My friend and mentor, Dr. Roland Sullivan, travels around the world urging and appealing to organizations to get ready for a tsunami of change that will come about in the next few years. He predicts silicon chips will be like second skin to humans; technology will not just change human intelligence but also match human emotion; and ethics in a digitalized world will move from just algorithms to human rhythms.

The possibilities of change are humongous and mind-blowing. Those who claim to be at the cutting edge of knowledge and technology cannot even fathom what will hit them in the face less than a decade from now.

Below is a short list of the effects on sales and selling of today's technology and social networking.

- Your customer knows a lot about your product and service; sometimes, even more than you do.

- They are often aware of what direction and which solution will work for them.

- They come prepared with what kind of money they want to spend and what kind of transactions or business partnerships they want.

All this has come about with the advent of the internet and the explosion of social media and social networking. Again, **the HeART of the CLOSE**, can only give you tips and insights

on how to get on this new wave. How do we ride and conquer this new wave? Well, we will all just have to wait until tomorrow.

THE HEART OF SOCIAL SELLING

To say that selling is a social exchange is an understatement. Selling is a human interaction and, thus, always has been social. Think of a flea market. Think of a fresh food, organic market. How do people move, talk, and interact? They impress each other through authenticity, quality offerings and respect as well as by forging relationships and providing value for the customer.

Selling on social media and social networks is similar in many ways but it is amplified and augmented by technology applications and platforms like Twitter, YouTube, LinkedIn, Facebook, and Instagram. It's a huge marketplace but instead of walking through on foot, you navigate by tapping fingers on the silicon screen. What's so amazing is you can cover greater distances in a shorter time. What's not so great is we can get bogged down by the novelty and the technology. And what's more, technology and the corresponding novelty are constantly changing.

Regardless of its speed, size and humongous ambiguity, *the HeART of the CLOSE* remains authentic on social media and social networks and maintains its value creation by building relationships with care. If you are one of the millions who think the buying process is going to change faster than the selling philosophies and processes well, you are right. If you believe that you, as a selling professional, will have to move forward in leaps and bounds, you are also correct.

the HeART of the CLOSE

Here are five powerful insights on selling in a digital world to help you move forward.

1. Prospect and discover customers and market opportunities through social media.

Keep your ear on the constantly changing ground by: (a) using alerts such as TweetDeck, Google, and the Cloud to let you know where your target client is; (b) listen in to your target clients' concerns and the outcomes they are seeking and participate in online discussions; (c) offer genuine information and insights without pushing your services or your brand.

2. Practice patience and consistency towards building your brand.

Think of the social media and its many networks as a patch of forestry filled with a variety of birds singing a variety of songs. Those who you want to seek you out will need to warp their hearing and listening skills to locate you and trust that you will be there when they reach out for you. But even in a dynamic marketplace abuzz with a myriad of constantly changing sums and offers, a certain kind of consistency will stand out and provide stability, credibility and certainty.

Write blogs toward a single theme. Tweet information and news about that theme or clearly related subjects. Post updates at regular days and times.

3. Follow through with the exact product or service you created a buzz about.

Truth in advertising they used to call it. Grapevine or Word of

the HeART of the CLOSE

Mouth Marketing it was called in recent years. It is now as it was in the olden days. It is also how it'll always stay. You just cannot get away with doing things wrong. My friend and mentor Sidney, used to say "Trash always surfaces." So no matter how good your pitch, your presentation or the buzz you create if your service doesn't match your claims the world will quickly boot you out.

4. Ensure that every buzz, bite, or pixel of information you put out on the Internet space represents the value proposition you offer.

No customer likes walking into a store that claims to sell quality shoes only to find they don't even carry shoes, so be authentic in your advertising on social media.

5. Exceed expectations. A better strategy would be not just to match and represent your promotion but to always surpass the promise you make.

Sometime ago, I heard Anthony Robbins share a story of how at a party one evening in Los Angeles, California a woman threw a tantrum when she couldn't order pizza anywhere at past midnight. She then decided to call her favourite online shoe store Zappos.com.

Just as she was about to phone Zappos, its owner and CEO Tony Hsieh, who happened to be at the party, contacted his chief-of-staff with instructions to support and serve the pizza-craving woman at the party who had called Zappos for a pizza. Well, the story ended with the wish of the pizza-craving woman being turned into reality by a shoe-selling company who stood by their promise of providing the best customer service possible.

CO-CREATING VALUE FOR THE WORLD

Some 15 years ago, I was at a sales seminar in Manila, Philippines run by a very experienced colleague in the sales training industry. He began by stating that in his 20 years of experience in selling and in teaching selling skills, nothing much had changed. He claimed sales is the same as in the past and will always remain the same.

From the audience, I disagreed with him and claimed that at that time, 15 years ago, selling had become faster, better, and cheaper because of the new technologies then. I claimed our reach as sales professionals has increased and the possibilities have multiplied. We no longer had to pedal our wares from the back of our carriage or our truck. We no longer had to wear our shoes out, carry brochures and samples in our bags or knock on people's doors. My trainer friend, with a serenely wise smile on his face, gave in to my argument and went on running his class.

Today, I suspect that my friend absolutely knew that someday I would discover and learn that selling in its core goes beyond prospecting, pitching, presenting and closing. And neither is it only about being faster, better and cheaper. Selling at its heart is about creating value for your customer, and the revenues and profits are the by-product, the fringe benefits of the service you provide which created value for your customer. That essence of selling has not changed and will remain the same, but the approach has evolved into an enhanced synergy. While creating value for your customers, selling has become a process of co-creation in partnership with our customers to provide value for the world.

the HeART of the CLOSE

Across the world, sales professionals now take up desk and office space within their customer's premises and work hand in hand with their customer's Product Development, Production, and Logistics Departments. Together, they research to create products and services that will make the world a better place with every close. The sales professional of today knows a close does not mean the end. It signals a new beginning.

A close does not mean the end.
It signals a new beginning.

the HeART of the CLOSE

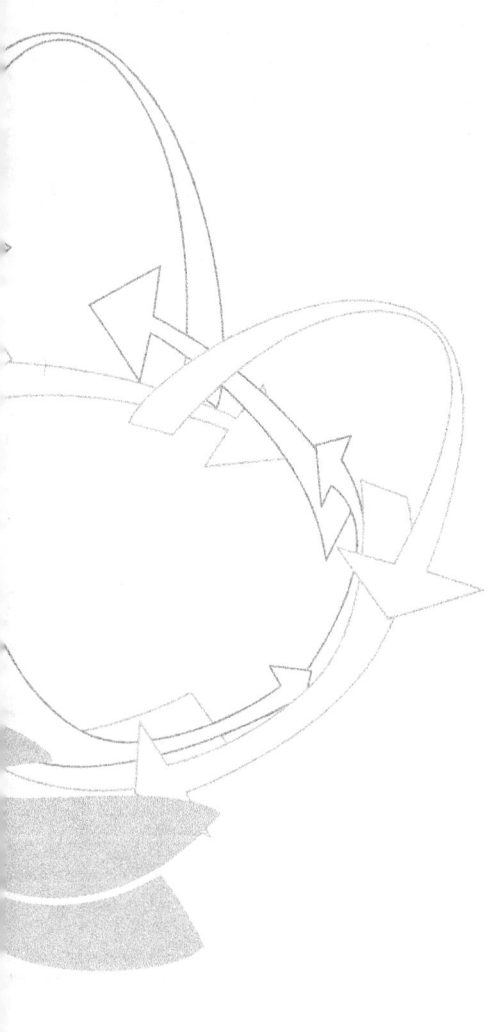

INDEX

INDEX

REFERENCES

1. **Primal Leadership**, 2002   Daniel Goleman
2. **Neuromarketing**, 2007 Patrick Renvoise and Christophe Morin
3. **Samurai Selling**, 1994 by Chuck Laughlin
4. **NLP Business Masterclass**, 2001   David Molden
5. **From Coach to Awakener**, 2003 Robert Dilts
6. **What the Customer Wants You to Know**, 2007 Ram Charan
7. **SPIN Selling**, 1988 Neil Rackham
8. **The New Strategic Selling**, 2005 Robert B. Miller and Stephen E. Heiman
9. **The New Conceptual Selling**, 2005 Robert B. Miller and Stephen E. Heiman
10. **The 250 Sales Questions to Close the Deal**, 2005 Stephan Schiffman
11. **Sun Tzu Strategies for Selling**, 2004 Gerald A. Michaelson with Steven W. Michaelson
12. **Intuitive Selling**, 2004 Thomas Wood-Young
13. **The Secrets of Great Sales Management**, 2004 Robert A. Simpkins
14. **Bag the Elephant**, 2008 Steve Kaplan
15. **How to Negotiate Anything with Anyone Anywhere Around the World**, 2008 Frank I. Acuff
16. **Ultimate Sales Tool Kit**, 2007 William "Skip" Miller
17. **The Art of Social Selling**, 2014 Shannon Belew
18. **Consultative Closing**, 2007 Greg Bennett

ABOUT INNER SUN

We at Inner Sun believe that every individual and every organization is a living system. At any given moment in this living system, there are three dimensions continuously at play.

The first is the dynamism that is innate, congenital, and embedded. In an individual, it is sometimes referred to as nature or personality; in a business organization, it may be referred to as "work culture".

The second dynamism is the one that exists outside of this system and is of many forms; the way that it is often referred to is the environment, economy, or ecology.

The third, the most vibrant, with a high potential to influence the inner and the outer dynamisms, is the dynamics of the process between the internal and external systems. The drivers of this intermediate dynamism are awareness, intelligence, emotion, memory, and action.

Inner Sun, the organization, focuses its own awareness, intelligence, and action towards this intermediary dynamism in all endeavors and interventions. The guiding elements behind our endeavors and interventions are:
- **Clarity** of thought, words, and action;
- **Creativity** of design, approach, and strategy; and,
- **Conscientiousness** of purpose and ultimate objectives.

the HeART of the CLOSE

Thinking free of bias and mental hammerlocks leads to higher clarity, creativity, and conscientiousness. As individuals and organizations strive for that status, their intelligences expand, interests broaden, and achievements soar.

We provide:
- Business solutions and interventions that bring about measurable results;
- Trainers who judge success not on their own performances but by how much the delegates learn;
- Personal service and tons of great value in an atmosphere of inspiration, support, and motivation;

ABOUT THE AUTHOR

Raju Mandhyan is a Cross-Cultural Leadership Coach, Workplace Learning Professional and Keynote Speaker. Businesses, teams, and individuals have benefitted for over fifteen years now from change consultancy, capability enhancement, and coaching services provided by his organization.

He has written books on communication skills, business leadership and engagement.   His work is inspired by the disciplines of Appreciative Inquiry, Open Space Technology and Neuro-Linguistic Programming. He has lived and worked in three different cultures—Indian, American and Filipino and now lives and works out of the Philippines.

OTHER PUBLICATIONS BY RAJU MANDHYAN

Many of these are available at leading bookstores in India, the Philippines and on Amazon.

The HeART of Public Speaking, 256 Pages, Published in 2005
Use Tony Buzan's Mind Mapping techniques to re-search, organize and deliver all kinds of presentations with style and dexterity.

The Heart of Humor, 200 Pages, Published in 2007
Employ clean and relevant humor to build rapport and then lead.

Pit Bulls and Entrepreneurs, 120 Pages, Published in 2010
Five ferocious insights that spell business success!

The HeART of STORY, 165 Pages, Published in 2015
Connect, Engage and Influence your audiences and your world through the creative power of organizational and inspirational storytelling.

Raju Mandyan's books on Amazon: http://goo.gl/OZSMj8
Posts on Facebook: https://goo.gl/MXQEqU
Talks on You Tube: https://goo.gl/dVclfm
Choice Clips from TV Show, ExPat InSights :   https://www.youtube.com/watch?v=vjf3sHaZBSo

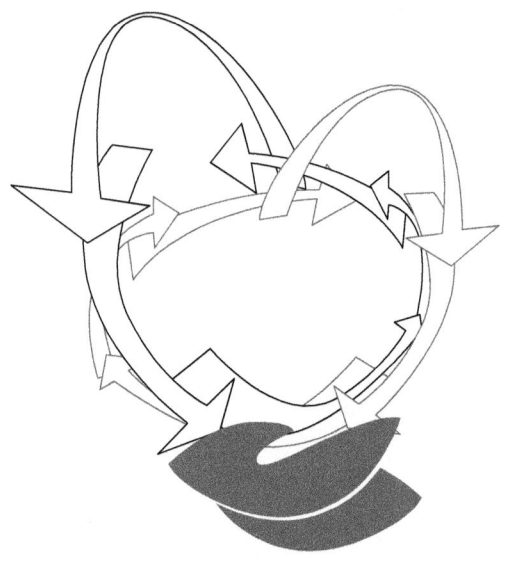

www.ingramcontent.com/pod-product-compliance
Lightning Source LLC
Chambersburg PA
CBHW051901170526
45168CB00001B/191